# Life Cycles

# Life Cycles

## Women and Pastoral Care

EDITED BY ELAINE GRAHAM
AND MARGARET HALSEY

First published in Great Britain 1993
Society for Promoting Christian Knowledge
Holy Trinity Church
Marylebone Road
London NW1 4DU

British Library Cataloguing-in-Publication Data
A catalogue record for this book is available from the British Library
ISBN 0–281–04688–3

Typeset by Ponting–Green Publishing Services, Chesham, Bucks
Printed in Great Britain at the University Press, Cambridge

# Contents

# Contents

# The Contributors

**Elaine L. Graham** is lecturer in social and pastoral theology at the University of Manchester. She previously worked as a regional officer for the Student Christian Movement, and as lay ecumenical chaplain to Sheffield City Polytechnic. Her particular interest is in the development of a feminist pastoral theology. She is currently completing doctoral research on the significance of gender studies for pastoral practice.

**Margaret J. Halsey** works for the Industrial Mission in South Yorkshire as industrial chaplain in Rotherham. She previously worked for the Christian Education Movement, and later as lay Anglican chaplain to Brighton Polytechnic. Her dissertation for her diploma in counselling explored the contribution which the women's movement has made to counselling and therapy. As part of a master's degree in the theological understanding of industrial society, she is currently researching changing patterns of women's work.

**Hazel Addy** is a minister in the United Reformed Church (URC). Formerly chaplain to Manchester University, she now works as national AIDS adviser for the URC.

**Thelma Aldcroft** gained midwifery experience in Glasgow and Salford before sharing with Malcolm the births and parenting of Frances, Kate, and Martin. She then worked as a Relate counsellor in Wakefield, and is currently a health visitor.

**Jan Berry** is ecumenical chaplain to Sheffield Hallam University. She previously worked for twelve years as a team minister in Baptist/URC churches in the Manchester area. She is a member of Women In Theology, and at the time of writing is its Chair. She is excited by developing new forms of material for liturgy and worship. Her previous publications include *Words for Worship*, WIT, 1992; *Naming Ourselves – a Feminist Re-Telling of Gospel Stories*, WIT, 1992. Other material appears in Morley, J., (ed.) *Bread for Tomorrow*, SPCK, 1992.

**Sandra Freeman** lectures at the University of Sussex in French, and sexual dissidence and cultural change. She is also a playwright, and has had several plays performed on the London Fringe, and for radio.

**Barbara A. Harrison** is an Anglican deacon working in the Sheffield Manor Local Ecumenical project. She was formerly Anglican chaplain to the University of York.

**Barbara Harrison** is assistant curate at St Andrew's Church, Immingham, South Humberside. **Penelope Harrison** is a graduate of the University of Manchester in theology and religious studies.

**Celia Hart** trained at Brighton Polytechnic in visual communication. She has worked for an educational publisher, and is now a freelance designer and illustrator.

**Karen Kennedy** lives with her husband and son in Liverpool, where they attend the local meeting of the Religious Society of Friends. Her paid work is as a Lecturer in adult basic education.

**Liz Kirby** is a teacher, poet, and mother, at present living in Macclesfield. She has done a variety of jobs, from working with children with disabilities, to leading writing workshops on relating to the environment with a local action group. At present she teaches at Stoke-on-Trent sixth-form college and writes in her spare time. Her poem 'Nativity' has been published in *The Collins Book of Contemporary Christian Verse*, and 'Seventh Day' in *Slow Dancer* magazine.

## The Contributors

**Ann Lewin** taught for many years, and is now welfare assistant in the students' union at the University of Southampton. She writes, leads quiet days and retreats, and is a local tutor for the Southern Diocesan Ministerial Training Scheme.

**Faith O'Reilly** trained as an artist at the Royal Academy in London, taught art in secondary and higher education, and now spends time painting in France. She helped to found the Stanley Spencer Gallery in Cookham, Berkshire.

**Alison Peacock** lives in Manchester, and at the time of writing works as a research associate at the William Temple Foundation. She has a master's degree in adult education from the University of Sheffield, and has a special interest in women in part-time higher education. Earlier, she received a comprehensive education in central Scotland.

**Elizabeth Nash** worked as a local minister for the URC in Manchester, Bolton, and Rotherham for sixteen years. Since 1979, she has been employed as a member of the Industrial Mission in South Yorkshire. She was moderator of the Industrial Mission Association from 1987–91.

**Susan F. Parsons** is principal of the East Midlands Ministry Training Course. She was born in the United States, and came to Britain to work on a PhD in contemporary theological ethics. She has taught in various institutions, and was a lecturer at Nottingham Polytechnic before joining the staff of EMMTC. She is married, with a son.

**Jill Robson** works for the Department of Employment researching into changing patterns of work. She previously worked in adult theological education.

**Margaret Selby** is director of training in the Diocese of Sheffield. Her previous pastoral experience includes work in varieties of ministry in parishes, education, and community relations.

## The Contributors

**Hilary Thomas** has eight years' experience as a social worker in Manchester and Sheffield, and is currently working in an urban priority estate as a member of a child care team. She is married to a clergyman, and they have three sons.

**Heather Walton** is tutor in society at Northern Baptist College, Manchester and has also worked as a researcher for the Methodist Church and for the Student Christian Movement. She is currently researching for a PhD in feminist theology and modernist women's fiction, and is co-editing a collection of women's sermons.

# Introduction

This collection of essays explores how women who give and receive pastoral care may contribute to a new understanding of Christian faith and practice. It pays particular attention to different aspects of the lifecycle, from cradle to grave, and uses the specific experiences of women from different situations to explore how a more appropriate pastoral practice may be developed. This is of concern not just to the churches – although this is primarily a book about Christian pastoral care – but has implications for social and public policy as well.

The concrete and particular changes and developments in women's lives provide the starting-point for our reflections. However, this book is also concerned to explore the extent to which the specific may be of relevance in a more general context. Thus, the stories speak from a particular situation, but also transcend the limits of their own circumstances, towards a broader understanding of their implications. The essays move from the immediate to the corporate, from experience to analysis, and from practice to theory.

Such a perspective is part of a broader understanding of the significance of context for Christian thought and practice. Over the past generation, voices have been emerging that argue strongly and persuasively for an approach to the Christian faith that emphasizes the primacy of the local, the specific, and the experiential for theological thought and practice. This understanding inevitably involves a recognition of the diversity of human experience. The Christian community is acknowledging its own plurality on a global scale, realizing that it can no longer speak with one voice. In the last decades of the twentieth century, there has been a proliferation of theologies, which serve to articulate the perspectives of groups like women, peoples of the 'Two-Thirds World', the poor, disabled, and powerless.

As one example of this process, feminist theologians argue that the mainstream Christian tradition has historically marginalized and discounted the perspectives of women. The androcentric nature of theology has often presumed that one group of humanity can represent universal human experience and speak on behalf of others. By exposing the dangers and distortions of this assumption, and integrating the experiences and understandings of women, feminist theology envisages that the Christian tradition can be renewed.

## Christian pastoral care

Although the dominant contemporary image of pastoral care is that of one-to-one counselling, it is more fully understood – certainly in historical perspective – as all those activities which contribute to the care, support, and development of the Christian community as a whole. As these essays testify, pastoral care increasingly is understood as practised through activities as diverse as worship, spiritual direction, collective action, and social ministry; all forms of Christian practice which aim to enable individuals and groups to grow more completely into a life of faith.

The aims of this book are therefore three-fold: first, to identify aspects of women's experience of giving and receiving pastoral care, hitherto ignored or hidden; second, to set these in the context of women's lives in contemporary church and society; and third, to envisage how new models of pastoral care might emerge, or are already emerging, from women's critical perspectives and from their reappropriation of traditional patterns of pastoral care.

This book begins the process of recovering areas of women's lives which have not formerly been considered within Christian pastoral care. The contributors aim to name those experiences often denied or silenced, and to highlight those dimensions of pastoral practice and need which have traditionally been neglected. Differences between women – be they of colour, race, culture, sexuality, class, or nationality – should alert us to the impossibility of universalizing or generalizing about women's lives. Instead, they speak from a variety of specific standpoints, as a reminder that pastoral care is grounded in the particular and concrete relationships and activities of everyday life.

Several contributors explore how appropriate pastoral care involves articulating and responding to aspects of women's experience which have hitherto been hidden. In preparing these essays for publication, we have realized that the process of bringing women's experience into the public domain is far from straightforward. For example, it is ironical that some women who were approached to contribute to this book found the demands of a lifestyle which involved caring for others precluded them from writing.

## Speaking and silencing

During the preparation of this book, the publisher's governing body took the decision not to proceed with the publication of a collection of prayers and liturgies by and for gay and lesbian Christians, *Daring to Speak Love's Name*. As a result, some potential contributors felt it would not be appropriate to write for SPCK at this time. However, the editors and the majority of contributors believed the incident to be symptomatic of a more deep-seated conflict within the Church about the validity of non-conformist lifestyles.

The controversies which surrounded this decision identify an extensive agenda for a genuinely inclusive pastoral theology. Authentic pastoral care needs to reflect the reality of lived experience in all its complexity and diversity. This entails responding to, and learning from, the integrity of those whose perspectives have historically been excluded from the established Christian tradition. This volume is one part of a growing movement in which perspectives that have traditionally been disregarded are claiming the right to contribute to theological debate.

People who have the courage, and the opportunity, to articulate their experiences for the first time know only too well the risks of potential rejection, scepticism, and misunderstanding. This is true whether it occurs in the context of a publication, or within a pastoral relationship. Many involved in pastoral care would endorse the importance of respecting and hearing the experience of individuals; but in practice much of the institutional church 'hears' experience selectively and conditionally.

The principle of selective hearing is not only true of some of the circumstances which surrounded *Daring to Speak Love's Name*, but, in a different context, is relevant to many of the essays in this volume. As any pastoral carer knows, there is a world of difference between hearing a story and actively listening to the significance of what is being said. Several contributors to this collection identify the dissonance between the private lives and needs of women, and the norms which inform any public consensus about pastoral policy in the churches. Serious listening to the stories of those whose experiences are only now emerging into the public domain involves the critical examination of the dominant values which consciously or unconsciously guide Christian pastoral practice.

We are very aware that this volume is also selective in the range of women's experience it encompasses and explores. It can therefore only claim to represent the beginnings of a process in which women's experiences of giving and receiving pastoral care are to be heard and acknowledged, and might suggest priorities for personal, institutional, and theological change.

## Some ways of using this book

The essays have been selected to reflect a number of different styles, intending to express the diversity of women's experiences. It is anticipated that the material can be read and used in a variety of ways: as case studies for ministerial and pastoral education; as material for study and discussion groups; in academic study and research; or in the development of practical pastoral strategies. While each of the essays can be read and appreciated in their own right, several common themes emerge.

The articles have been grouped into four sections. Each of these brings together shared concerns, some of which are identified in the introduction to each section. Each section describes a particular stage in the process of naming women's experiences, developing a critique of existing models of pastoral response, and identifying the implications of and for a renewed theory and practice.

First, there is the task of enabling these experiences to be articulated, particularly where they have been hidden or repressed. One function of any form of care is to listen to and value people's basic needs and situations. Many of the essays illustrate the subtle ways in which women's experiences are often denied or trivialized. By enabling such stories to be heard, their reality can be respected and valued.

Second, it is important for these needs to be placed in a wider context: to interpret and analyse the underlying causes and dynamics of women's experiences. This involves taking such stories beyond the personal and immediate to see how social, cultural and historical factors have shaped them.

Third, the results of such analyses are brought into dialogue with traditional teachings and patterns of care. The book asks how adequately the received tradition meets the needs of women, and explores areas where a new synthesis of the historical and the contemporary may be required. The credibility of pastoral care lies in its ability to respond adequately to needs, and to meet whatever criteria of 'good practice' have been developed.

Fourth, the impact of transformed practices on the Christian tradition itself are discussed. Some implications for models of ministry, for patterns of worship and spirituality, and for an understanding of Scripture and Christian theology are considered. By offering new models of pastoral care and vocation, the voices and experiences of women giving and receiving care may make a significant and effective contribution to the wider Christian community.

Such a process is ultimately cyclical in serving to generate a renewed and inclusive pastoral strategy. Authentic pastoral care will always need to return to an immediate context of need, in order to test out and discover new practices. In the process it will elicit further stories and address further needs. Furthermore, the aims and objectives of this model are not directed towards isolated crisis management or once-and-for-all 'problem-solving'. Rather, they seek to develop a continuing process of supporting, challenging, and equipping people in their journey through the lifecycle.

# PART ONE

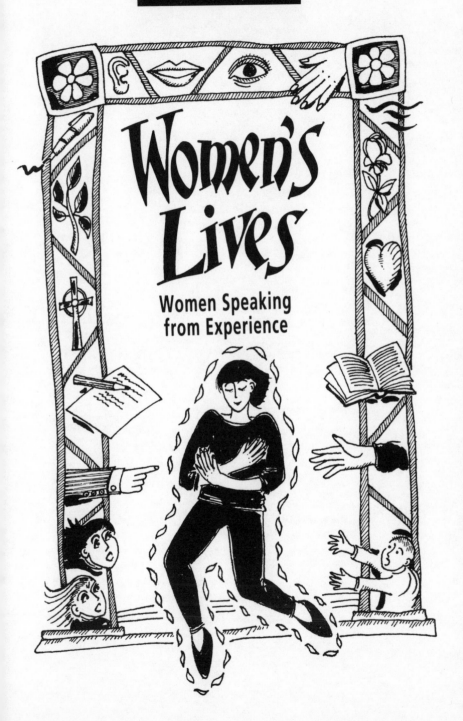

# WOMEN'S LIVES

## Women Speaking from Experience

This section contains five contributions which explore different aspects of women's experience throughout the lifecycle.

Karen Kennedy explores how her experience as a new mother created demands and opportunities which overturned previously held assumptions and expectations. She writes of the effects of being plunged into an unfamiliar and demanding role with little support or preparation, and of her struggle with the ambiguities and surprises of her new status.

Barbara and Penelope Harrison discuss the way in which their relationship as mother and daughter has affected their beliefs and values. Despite the divergences in their respective faiths, they are able to support one another as they continue to pursue their spiritual and personal quests.

Margaret Selby exchanges insights with two friends from different cultural and religious backgrounds, discovering much in common in terms of single women's struggle to maintain their integrity and vocation in the face of strong social pressures and conventions.

Ann Lewin also speaks about the mother-daughter relationship, but at a different stage in the lifecycle. Her experience of caring for her elderly mother raises questions about society's expectations that women will naturally and automatically exercise care, regardless of personal cost.

Faith O'Reilly's story is of a lesbian woman coming to terms with her sexuality and identity in a cultural and religious context which offered little in the way of positive role models or support. By finding greater affirmation and integrity through the creative arts, she has been able to combine self-expression with collaborative work in fostering the creative gifts of others.

A common theme in all these contributions is the tension between autonomy and dependence. Traditionally, women are taught that self-fulfilment comes through serving others, and identity is found in relationships. These essays uncover the conflicts such expectations generate – often at the expense of individual autonomy and wellbeing.

# 1 *The Unwritten Journal*

KAREN KENNEDY

## *One month*

Before my son arrived, I harboured fantasies of rediscovering the creative part of myself that seemed to have become submerged under pressures of paid work. I would sew curtains, decorate the house, and make a patchwork quilt. I now realize that babies take up *all* your time. They may sleep sometimes – but when they do you rush round the house clearing up all the mess they have left for you – rinse nappies, clothes on the line, change soaked T-shirt. Suddenly, my time is no longer my own; it belongs completely to somebody else.

My life has adopted my son's rhythm and time is no longer governed by clocks, deadlines, or appointments. No more rushing to different parts of the city, grabbing lunchtimes in between. There is instead a constant but strangely satisfying tiredness. My obligations are clear-cut and mostly a pleasure: to keep the baby, myself, and occasionally my partner fed and clean and dry. When there is any time left over, sleep is the top priority. For once in my life, sleep is not an effort: a few minutes lying down and I am out like a light.

Admittedly, sitting down for forty-five minutes while being milked by an ever-gorging baby can become rather boring. Sometimes I wish we had a remote control for the TV. An outing to the shops up the road is a major event, seldom achieved before four o'clock. A visit anywhere else can only be timed roughly within the hour to accommodate possible all-change-nappy-situations, or yet another feed. Did anyone ever tell me that looking after a small baby involves more hours and work than the prime minister spends running the country, or did I just not hear?

Everyone expects a mother to be the expert when it comes to her child. In fact, I have never felt so de-skilled in

10

my life. It is very strange to feel such a complete novice, both in the art of parenting and the care of my child in particular. There are many times when he is crying and I don't know what is wrong. It has to be worked out by a process of elimination: nappy change? wind? feed? cuddle? walk up and down stairs in the baby sling?

## Two months

I looked at my feet today: my toenails had become talons. When on earth were they last cut? One of the many little jobs that just fall by the wayside. Oh, for a long soak in the bath, with time to pluck my eyebrows, cut my nails, rub in body lotion! If I do get to the bath I never stay in very long because I can hear D. crying downstairs. In fact, I don't really relax at all if D. is in the house. I collapse in a heap of relief if somebody offers to take him for a walk, and revel in the delicious peace of a quiet, undisturbed house now that I need not keep one ear ready and alert. There are so many things I miss from that time when I had freedom: reading a whole newspaper article, watching an entire TV programme, drinking a cup of tea or eating in peace, reading books, leisurely walks round the shops, uninterrupted chats, doing the ironing, time just to sit and gaze at the ceiling.

For some, the path of Christ means self-renunciation to the will of God. First-time mothers are flung into a situation where they have little choice in the matter of self-renunciation. This can be difficult for those who, like me, have been brought up to expect a life of their own. I am reminded of the parable of the pearl of great price. There is an irredeemable price involved in having a child – a part of my life which is gone forever. However, what I gain in return is so precious as to be well worth the sacrifices.

Sometimes the anger within me catches me by surprise. Luckily, I have not felt any of the depression felt by other women, but I rage inside at my lack of freedom. I can't take it out on an innocent, defenceless baby, so I take it out on my partner. After all, *he* doesn't seem to have lost *his* freedom: he can stay on for a meeting at work, go for a drink on the way home, and even read the paper on a

Saturday morning; he doesn't have to account for the time he spends away from D., or make child care arrangements when he isn't there. The child within me rages at the unfairness of it all. But do I also detect within the anger a sense of loss and grief for the life I have lost, when I could take active decisions on how to use my time, and boogie the night away on a mere whim? There is grief, too, for the loss of the simple two-way partnership which has become such a complicated triangle.

When I ask B., my partner, how he does it, he says he 'makes time'. He takes his time when he wants it. I seem to snatch moments out of my child's time. If I think back to Mary and Martha, I have to admit that he has a point. Is it Martha, 'distracted by many tasks', whose incessant voice stops me from sitting down and attending to my inner needs? This voice too needs to be quietened, and, like Mary, I need to be given permission to be still.

On the other hand, these times are not without their spiritual moments. I have been amazed at how many people have shared in the joy of our child's birth. My parents' friends, my mother-in-law's neighbours, and my sister-in-law's colleague's mother have all sent presents. The ripples of this 'good news' have spread wide. I find too that the image of God as parent has taken on a new meaning as I am sometimes overwhelmed by the feelings I have for D. and suffer with every cry of pain he utters. Is this really the way we too are loved?

I have felt quite isolated from the Friends Meeting we attend. We have intended to go sometimes and been defeated by D.'s routine: he is usually working up to a feed by 11 am. Tolerant as Quakers are, I'm not sure how they would react to me breastfeeding during Meeting!

It feels as though I am having to cope with a major role-change at a time when the workload involved gives me little time to reflect on the experience, or even share my thoughts and feelings. It is important to me that there are people around who can empathize with my situation and share in the dilemmas, especially those who are at the same stage of apprenticeship themselves. It is also important to be receiving practical support. One student tells how she would not have coped with the early months if a cousin had not insisted on coming round once a week to babysit while she got away for a few hours. We should not feel ashamed that as carers we need to be cared for. This is one time in our lives when we need to be able to accept support, and to be assertive about our personal needs.

## Three months

I was creative today: I hung two pictures up in the hall! It felt so satisfying to have achieved a permanent change in the environment rather than just be attempting to stem the regular tide of dirty chaos.

My mind seems to operate in the same way as a busy newsroom. There is a constant list of things to do buzzing in my ear, and the running order changes as the circumstances of the day change. One minute I'm ahead of schedule and am planning to sit down with a cup of tea. The next, I notice a rather sticky child and everything stops so he can be changed and bathed, and the resulting laundry soaked and washed in an ever-repeating routine.

My mother seemed to find time to knit layettes, make bibs and dresses. She also washed out all my nappies by hand. I think this must have been a miracle of coping, especially as she went back to work as a full-time junior doctor, night duty and all, when I was three months old. On the other hand, we were filled up with National dried-milk powder, and on solids at four weeks, so at least we slept through the night. We were also wrapped up and wheeled out in the back in our prams, whatever the weather, to sleep and look at the sky.

Fortunately, I also know about the time when the three of us were young and the vicar came to call. There were empty milk bottles on the mantelpiece and dirty nappies on the floor. I find this episode very reassuring. It gives me permission not to be on top of everything all the time.

## Four months

Returning to paid employment, albeit on a part-time basis, is playing havoc with my concepts of work and leisure. Work is sometimes my escape, my social life, even my relaxation. It makes me feel like a normal human being. Pushing D. round the park should fit under the category of leisure, but my main aim is to encourage him to sleep. Family outings can be the most stressful activities of all because they require so much preparation. Nappy-bag, drink, food, change of clothes all have to be prepared for even the shortest outing. Shopping is supposed to be a leisure activity, but I'd prefer to clean the bathroom: at least I can see some evidence of what I've achieved at the end.

On the other hand, my time management skills have improved no end. I'm usually an habitual procrastinator, never doing today what could be left until the last minute. I can now predict with a fair amount of accuracy the times during the week when I'll be able to work on lesson preparation, so it has to be done there and then. If it's left it won't get done at all. Time is so precious, I'm annoyed with myself if I idle some of it away, or if other people waste it. I arranged to meet a colleague the other day about a new class, and she was half an hour late. She ought to realize how much it costs me in terms of organization and frayed nerves to arrive somewhere on time.

We've finally managed to attend our Friends Meeting a couple of times with D. Although I find it hard to still myself with D. there, he has in fact been quite good. People are quite appreciative of his gurgling noises, and they seem to add a new dimension to the silence. Upon reflection, perhaps Quakers are more accepting of small children than other churches where there is a set routine and we would worry about him drowning out the sermon. I feel that D. is valued for his role within the meeting, and ministry can be fitted into the quiet times.

*Five months*

A colleague today told me she lost four years of her life while she looked after her three young children, who were born quite close together. She was even hospitalized for exhaustion. In a way, she lost that part of her children's lives too because she had no time just to enjoy being with them. Of course, she also had to keep the house clean and have a meal on the table for when her husband came in. I'm constantly amazed at the way in which mothers cope with more than one child, entirely on their own, or without family close by. We cope because there's no room for failure – except perhaps the failure of our own nerves, marriages, or hearts.

All the statistics on women and mental health, women and smoking, women and drugs make sense in a way they never did before. On the one hand, I celebrate our strength which enables us to cope, but on the other hand, I wonder, does it have to be this way? Do these years of young children need to be times of drudgery and isolation? Because so many women go through this experience it is perceived as an inevitable part of motherhood and therefore normal. Normalization results in a devaluing of the suffering involved.

It isn't as if these observations on the experiences of women are anything new. They have been chronicled in literature, statistics, sociological surveys, and feminist analyses much more eloquently than they have been here. Is it that we don't really hear what's going until we experience it ourselves? And if this is true, what are the implications for theological investigation? If theology is to be rooted in experience, if it's to address real need, it can't be inferred from second-hand analysis. Even Jesus didn't use the mother-child relationship as a paradigm in his teaching. There are few biblical images to which I can directly relate the experience of motherhood. So should theology be created by the real experts – the mothers themselves?

## Eight months

At this point I have to come clean and admit that I don't think of motherhood as a sacred vocation. It just so happens that biological considerations have been extended by the structures in society as the most convenient way of organizing childcare. Though emotionally the Martha Complex may govern my ever-present feelings of responsibility, I'm fortunate in harbouring an inner certainty that motherhood doesn't necessarily entail total self-sacrifice and self-denial. Like anyone else, I'm influenced by upbringing, church, society, and Bisto adverts. However, my vision of what might be within our family means there are both inner and outer conflicts as we try to take what we want from tradition and work on our own alternatives to the stereotypes. What is faith about if it isn't vision?

I'm very glad that his mother isn't the only significant other in D.'s life, and that he's equally happy with his father or his grandmother. I don't feel guilty about leaving him while I'm at work, or even while I escape for a weekend. However, there's still a niggling sense of the primacy of the mother, as I'm still the one who spends the most time with him. I still consider myself the expert where he is concerned, and find it hard to accept somebody else's routine might suit him just as well as mine. I become disproportionately annoyed if the details of his life are not organized in the way I like. Does this betray insecurity on my part?

Whatever my ideals, feelings of guilt are still a constant companion. Am I asking too much of the other carers in his life? Should I be giving him more of my undivided attention instead of washing the dishes? Should I have left him on the living-room floor for a few moments while I go to the loo? According to the scriptures of Penelope Leach, this last action is definitely a sin, as baby should never be left alone for even a moment once he or she is the least bit mobile. They are all watching me – the child care experts, the health professionals, and the other mothers – to see if I attain their performance criteria.

Then there is the sensation of having to parcel myself out in so many directions that there isn't enough of me to go round. No wonder I continually question the proportions I give to each role, and feel guilty when B. says we don't have time for spontaneity anymore. Even leisure time has to be carefully measured out to be spent in the various permutations of our family relationship. We have nuclear family outings, visits to B.'s family, visits from my family, and outings separately with our own friends. B.'s mother also reminds us to have outings as a couple and offers to babysit, but these sometimes seem the most difficult to organize.

16

## Ten months

Sometimes it seems we have an ever-running battle over housework and child care. B. thinks that compared to other men he shares a good portion of the burden – which is true. I think, because he'll never do as much as me, he isn't doing enough. We get stuck in our parallel grooves of nagged husband and martyred wife. But it is more than this. We *(1993)* live at a particular point in history where expectations of men in the home and of women are changing. Both of us had working mothers, and saw what the burden of combining work and household responsibility did to them. We want our family to be different, but we do not have a role model for the father who takes his share of the responsibility, or a mother who lets go of hers. This is where the personal really becomes political, where we 'struggle to live out justice in our lives'.

I have been asked to consider working full-time. This has provoked a degree of internal conflict I didn't expect. Here is the opportunity I've been waiting for to launch my career and ascend from the ranks of the underdog part-timers. An ambitious streak urges me forward, but my intuition holds me back. These early years with D. are unrepeatable and I want to be able to enjoy them. Full-time employment would also place great stress on our life as a family. I don't like this conclusion, but it's unavoidable. I'm prepared to sacrifice my principles, but I'm not prepared to sacrifice the quality of my life.

Sometimes I wonder if I'm asking too much of life, if I want to have my time and eat it too. B. would really appreciate the opportunity to spend more time with his son, and I'm fortunate in having a satisfying job which does not take up all my time, an unproblematic child, and a mother-in-law who enjoys looking after him.

## Eighteen months

If you are wondering how I managed to write this journal if my experience was really as I described, then you have uncovered my conceit. The truth is that although I wanted to write down many of these thoughts at the time, I never quite got round to it. The thought of being published has been the main incentive for doing so now. In fact, writing this piece has been a feat in itself, as time has been snatched in between other responsibilities and I escaped to a friend's house for a weekend to allow a period of uninterrupted concentration.

So I have created a patchwork, though one quite different from the one I intended. Perhaps I've included too many of the darker patterns and not given a true impression of the whole. However, these were the parts that needed to be written through, as a therapeutic as well as creative act. Writing has helped me to analyse and come to terms with the experience. My choice has also been influenced by the message I wanted to convey to you, the reader, because I want you to take seriously the emotional and practical, as well as spiritual, needs of mothers.

We all work at creating balance in our lives. Perhaps for most of us, when it is achieved, it is a precarious balance. However, many women feel they are performing a balancing act which is nothing compared to that of a monocyclist juggling with five plates. Maybe some chaos is inevitable, but it seems to me there must be better ways of valuing both mothers and children, of sharing the responsibilities, and supporting the carers.

# 2 Conversation Piece

BARBARA and PENELOPE HARRISON

**Barbara:** I was brought up in a conservative church tradition where, in my teenage years, the young people who were my friends adopted the practice of proving their allegiance to Christianity by being willing to stand up and publically give their testimony. I used to go into the kitchen at those times, partly because I could not face standing up in front of others, and partly because I could not understand what they meant when they spoke of being 'saved'. Salvation seemed to be about access to a hidden knowledge rather than about restoration and wholeness in a process of healing.

At this early age, I encountered faith and spirituality as located outside myself in such a way as to devalue my inner thoughts, feelings and experiences of life. This adolescent experience of the denial of my inner self in the face of pressure to conform to the reality of the group, was closely linked to the failure to develop a sense of autonomy based on a self-esteem rooted deeply within the self. I grew up dependent on the affirmation of others.

For me, the task of later life has been focused on the reassessment and incorporation of that youthful experience, in a healing process towards integration and wholeness. Salvation has come to be understood as liberation from those childhood and adolescent experiences of insecurity that produced a lack of self-worth.

**Penelope:** It is strange to hear my mother talk of a time when she was insecure. She seems always to have been there for support. In my own adolescence, I, too, felt very insecure; likewise, the different Church traditions that I experienced left me very confused about the nature and meaning of Christianity. However, as I developed my own spiritual awareness in an active process based on my own

19

experience, I began to recognize and accept the value of my self. Through our joint experience, which is a generation apart, I can see adolescent insecurity as a common experience of women. However, my mother taught me to value rather than to deny my own experience, so that I do not feel alone in my journey: it is part of our relationship.

**Barbara:** When I was young, I was interested in what I now know to be theology, though at that time I took a history degree and followed a couple of courses in the theology faculty. What I heard and experienced in the Church hardly touched this interest. I could not make sense of it, and what is more I did not feel saved. It is only in later life that I have been able to put into words the images I brought from my teenage years, of Christ as a saviour figure. Christ was a knight in bright, shining armour, invulnerable, and sitting on a white charger with lance extended before him. He galloped towards me at full tilt, intent on saving me, from I know not what, and then he pulled up sharply in front of me. At that moment his chest exploded and blood pumped out all over me. That was how I had visualized salvation, and until my late thirties I had never realized that I was carrying those images inside me. I was supposed to feel saved, but what I actually felt was horror, and the feeling that I did not want anyone to sacrifice himself for me in that way. I was not worth it. It reinforced feelings of worthlessness.

**Penelope:** I, too, found the imagery surrounding Jesus and salvation alienating. I remember reading a children's book on the life of Jesus. On the last page there was a picture of the Crucifixion. I felt a deep pain as I realized the suffering that he undertook for me. Through my pain I felt angry. I did not ask him to do it. I could not refuse to worship God as this would show ingratitude for the pain that he had suffered for me. I felt as if I were being blackmailed.

By contrast, I encountered an alternative, more liberal Christianity which told us that God was everywhere; an immanent rather than a transcendent God. In Sunday school, run by my parents, we made lions out of toilet-roll tubes and acted in plays. It was fun. Religion and church-going were not forced on me. Nevertheless, I felt a deep confusion about the true essence of Christianity. I also felt a conflict between my own experiences and the Christian message, taught in books, that did nothing to affirm my experience.

**Barbara:** When Penelope was about ten years old, at the time when she was confirmed, I was struggling in a church that did not seem to offer me anything. There was a disparity between my own search for meaning and that offered by the Church. The denial of self, presented as the heart of true spirituality, reinforced my experience of non-being in life, where I only seemed to exist as a wife and a mother but not as an autonomous being. The spiritual life was still about the acquisition of knowledge; the words of the liturgy rendered me spiritually inarticulate, for there were no words or images that drew at all on how I was experiencing life. I had nothing to carry me forward from those images of adolescence into a spirituality for the life that I was now living.

**Penelope:** As a young girl growing up in the country, I had a deep awareness of the harmony of life. Many of my memories are of long, hot, summer days, walking in the deserted lanes, climbing trees, and splashing in the stream. Much of this I associated with the Church. I used to play the organ at the back of our small parish church, near a small window. I would look out of the window and see the rough grass, the green of the trees and hear the birds singing. The early morning sun reflected on the white walls of the church, which would be flooded with light. On Easter Sunday morning I played at another church in the parish. It was situated in the grounds of a large house, and inside it was small and musty with disuse. To me it felt like a lost hermitage, full of sacred mystery. Outside, walking up the path under the overhanging trees, I felt I was in the Easter garden, on the day of Resurrection. Life was all around me, and new life was emerging: this was Easter.

I had the same feelings inside the church. It was not just

21

a building set apart from the world, but part of nature. At harvest festival the walls would be lined with flowers and produce. Walking in from the autumn dusk, with its orange harvest moon, the church seemed vibrant with colour and noise. It was part of the harmony to which I belonged and of which I was a part. Since then I have discovered that this experience of the harmony with nature is shared by many women. This became the work of my dissertation in my final year at university.

It is said of women that we view the world as intimately related to ourselves. We experience our inner selves as connected to a greater power or sacred being. This being we see as immanent in us and revealed in nature. However, this nature is not some pastoral idyll, but is grounded in the realities of our lives. It is based in life and death, in our self-discovery through crises, and in our everyday lives. It is a spirituality not found in mainstream religious expression, which is conditioned by a masculine world-view. We must therefore develop our own authoritative texts, symbols, and liturgies to give our spirituality expression. In this process of awakening we can grow in who we are, and in response to the problems of our world. Although to identify women with nature may seem to be a traditional stereotype, it can liberate a woman's spirituality and a new way of being in the world.

**Barbara:** This connectedness with the world, which for Penelope was awakened through her love of nature, could not be articulated by me when I was her age. I could find no external authority for my feelings of oneness with the whole of creation when hanging out the washing on a misty autumnal morning, or when standing beneath the stars, or when absorbed in the vastness of the sea as it crashed upon the shore. If anything, they were to be regarded as anti-Christian.

The realization that such feelings had spiritual depth and were relevant to my life in the Church began to emerge in my experience of connection and relationship with my children. When my first child was born there was a moment when the world appeared to stand still; I and my daughter were at one with the heart of all that is. It was a highly symbolic and intensely religious moment of being in relationship with all things created and with the Creator of all. Here there was no division between the world of the spirit and that of the body, for this deeply spiritual moment arose out of an intensely physical process: the act of giving birth.

The search for meaning and purpose that began in my adolescence had always looked to external authority. Later, as I explored the imagery of birth, as living in and emerging from the womb, I discovered metaphors that spoke to my inner experience of life, and which provided illumination for the journey of integration and growth on which I had embarked in middle life. Experience became a source of authority, especially when it could be validated by the experience of others in biblical and spiritual traditions, subsumed by the dominant tradition.

The recovery of memory – remembering my own birth, childhood, and adolescence, reliving the pain of giving birth – have been a process of healing, in which I learned to accommodate the wounds of life and to integrate them into my life, rather than suppress them. However, I am conscious that my understanding of adolescent experience comes through the filter of this later healing process, and does not have the sense of urgency or immediacy that life has for my children.

**Penelope:** In adolescence the pain of living is very intense. There is no compromise when you are a teenager. Crises come thick and fast, and all situations appear to be of life and death. Looking back can therefore be very painful, remembering what now seems to have been mountains made out of molehills, and unnecessary surges of emotions. However, when we are young, the immediate pain does not seem to last as we hop from one situation to the next. Now as I look back, it seems distant: I remember the hurts of past situations without re-experiencing them. Remembering, as my mother has experienced it, is not relevant to my life now. Looking to the future is important, as we take the past with us but do not relive it. The pain of living is still present, and can be very intense, but the process of accommodating is a different one, without regrets or recrimination. Although the pain is not lost, the future possibilities are moving us on. So, the past is incorporated into my life as I quickly move on to living the present. Each of us sees our adolescence in relation to our present lives in a different way because we are at different stages of the lifecycle.

**Barbara:** Much later in life, in a release of my adolescent experience, I began to reinterpret the Crucifixion. I began to see it in terms of the wounds in my own life. I had been brought up to see Jesus as God in disguise, like one of the Greek gods assuming human form, so there was a sense in which the suffering had never been real or painful. Now, the Crucifixion came to have far more to do with entry into the depths of desolation that are a part of human living as we go through feelings of non-being: of only existing through others as a wife or a mother but not as an autonomous human being with a sense of self. The Crucifixion became a symbol for the presence of God in the realities of my life as a woman; a God who is present to me directly, rather than mediated through others.

Jesus, stripped of all the trappings with which my church had surrounded him, became a human being like me: all the perspectives changed. At that time I was reading *On Being a Christian* by Hans Küng, and there I found the external validation that gave me the courage to trust my own thoughts and feelings. The spiritual life became one of liberation into life. God ceased to be remote and became the life that creates, sustains and moves through all life, and the Resurrection the symbol of all that gives and nurtures life. I began to move away from images for God. Religious experience and spirituality became associated with the pool at the centre of my being: a wellspring that gurgled and bubbled away and sometimes sent up sparkling fountains. In the writings of Teresa of Avila, Hildegard of Bingen, and, especially, Meister Ekhardt, I found other companions for my journey and in the work of the feminist theologians an understanding of God that spoke directly to my experience.

**Penelope:** In secondary school I was encouraged to develop my experience of the harmony of life that I felt through my love of the natural world around me in rural Lincolnshire. In English lessons I was encouraged to observe and describe my environment. Here I could use my imagination freely to write about what I saw and felt. It was in these lessons that I learned to appreciate my surroundings and to enjoy my thoughts and feelings for them. I could articulate this feeling in my own way, for in English I was not restricted by what was considered 'appropriate' or 'authoritative' by the Church.

In my teenage years, I perceived Christianity as failing to speak to life as I experienced it, and so I rejected the Church's authority. My mother was a different authority figure, and we had long conversations together. She spoke to me about the importance of following my own insights in my own way. She affirmed my experience as being valuable and important. I realized that Christianity was not the only authority, and did not have to be accepted uncritically. I could question its authority without myself feeling rejected or guilty.

Validating authorities are important in our lives in order to affirm our present experience and to lead us into new ways of living. It is important to discover texts and expressions that speak to our own spiritual experience. In submitting uncritically to external pressures we may deny or negate our true selves. I experience Christianity as a religion which seems to be about moulding my spiritual experiences into a framework imposed upon me. As I develop a personal expression of my spirituality, I can rediscover a sense of self-autonomy. I can begin to see my life as a whole, living in a way that is compatible with my inner, holistic authentic, spiritual experiences, and not to an external ideal. As a young person, I think it is vital to gain the courage and commitment to live our lives from our sense of autonomy, not according to the dogmas of traditional authorities.

**Barbara:** What is important for both of us, mother and daughter, is that our experience became a shared experi-

ence and we empower one another. Our individual spiritual
quests, while taking us in different directions, have a
reciprocal quality to them. We can still share together and
support one another. As a deacon in the church, I do not
have to feel a failure because my daughter has found herself
elsewhere. I value what she has given and continues to give
to me, and am nourished by her. When life in the institutional church feels stultified and sterile, the long talks with
Penelope remind me of the spring that still bubbles away
and keeps me in touch with the God who will not be
confined within systems and structures.

**Penelope:** Life, especially when we are young, can seem full
of confusion and crises. However, life is to be lived and not
agonized over. This is not necessarily a shallow attitude;
rather, through living out our lives we discover meaning. In
discovering and developing our own experience we can
begin to live in a way that is authentic to us. The self-
autonomy that can be awakened through this is accompanied by responsibility. We have a responsibility to ourselves to carry through our new consciousness into practice.
But there is also a responsibility to our environment and to
the world as a whole. As we realize that we are interrelated
to this world, that we can change it as it can affect us, then
we must consider the effects of all our actions.

In living our life authentically, we must take the responsibility to carry through our new consciousness to that with
which we are in relationship. This includes not only our
friends and family, but also the world; a world which will
not become more free or just overnight. Self-realization
goes beyond ourselves, into taking responsibility for redefining all relationships. With the discovery of self-autonomy
we accept greater freedom, and with it the responsibility to
carry our awareness into all areas of life. We have to find
our own way of living out this new self-consciousness
without creating scapegoats for the problems that we face,
and thus we must consider our actions, and take responsibility for the effects.

Because of my questioning of Christian authorities, I
have come to reject the Church. I have discovered my own

traditions and texts that validate and legitimize my experience of the world and of the sacred. Through my mother's acceptance of this I have not encountered the demand for self-denial or the rejection that others may have felt. I have learned the importance of and the strength to be gained from following my own beliefs, in my personal relationships and in my relationship to the world. Finally, I have rejected traditional authorities because of their failure to speak to my spirituality; I would now say that I am not a Christian.

**Barbara:** For those of us who choose to remain within the Church, there needs to be a new understanding which breaks down the old divisions between Church and world in a spirituality that belongs, not to some separate realm, but affirms the life of this world. If we are to understand the encounter with God as both mediated and embodied, then the world is where we meet God, not just in material objects, but in the whole of life. This feminist vision is not an attempt to set up a countercult, but an attempt to bring women's insights to bear on mainstream theology and Church life. The intention is to provide us all, men and women, with a theology which will allow us to live in that tension between God's immanence and transcendence in such a way that we can respond to the divine love for us in loving responsibility for the whole of God's creation.

This means that we need to reappropriate those symbols for the spiritual life of giving birth, raising children and running a household that have been taken from us in a male-oriented Church, so that we can create liturgies that express the fullness of God in whose image both women and men are created. This is not to exalt mothering above fathering, but to restore the fullness of parenting.

The sacramental life of the Church for me provides a means of both expressing and experiencing the divine-human encounter in a way that reaches into the depths of our being, so that not only do we perceive God's gift of self, but we also express who we are before God. Questions about the use of gendered language in our sacramental liturgies have deep consequences. First, in expressing the full humanity of women and incorporating women's experience into the divine-human encounter; and second, in communicating the authority of God as both transcendent and also a close presence within our lives as men and women.

This emphasis on God as immanent in the world and in human community moves us away from God as supreme determining power to stress human freedom and responsibility in relationship. Salvation is then transformed from being about denial of self and feelings of worthlessness, to being about human liberation demonstrated in a mutuality of relationship that characterizes the unmerited love of the divine-human relationship. And redemption is concerned with the fulfillment of all humanity, not merely as individuals, but as community in the social and political realities of this world.

The God seen in and through the man Jesus does not stand aside from suffering humanity, but is identified with the suffering of humanity in the pain and oppression of this world. Thus the emphasis in my own spirituality is to encourage the values of inclusiveness, mutuality, wholeness, fulfillment, transformation, anticipation and celebration. This goes to build such a vision of redemptive community where all, women and men, young and old, have a part to play. As we enter into relationships and seek to live out our interrelatedness, one with another, and with the world around us, we encounter the God who is experienced within daily human life and in whom we all live.

# 3 *Being Single*

MARGARET SELBY *et al.*

In *The Fire and the Rose Are One* (Moore, 1980), the author says 'the universal human need in its fully adult form is the need "to be myself for another", with the word "for" referring both to my attraction to the other and the other's attraction to me.' For the unmarried, either by choice or by force of circumstances, such a quotation can be an unwelcome invitation to feel worthless, or 'to seek to be made to feel worthful by others', as Moore says.

However, it is possible for singleness to become 'the life-enhancement of another' or of others, as the correspondence between myself, G. – a Zulu woman in South Africa, and B. – an Indian Christian woman living in Britain – makes clear. Each of us had discussed our singleness at intervals over several years. It is clear from our letters that all three of us have had to work at letting it be the means of our own personal growth. There has, however, been an unexpectedness in our struggle towards maturity, because in each case, sometimes unperceived by ourselves, our singleness has become a source of strength for others. Especially in the other two cases, it has been a beacon of light and a strong challenge to the norms of society that inform women's marriage patterns, and can often end in life-denying relationships.

The letters between the three of us, written over six months, speak for themselves. They may also speak powerfully and prophetically to other people seeking to make sense of a single life. At best, they will be agents for others to accept their singleness positively and even joyfully, and may challenge people to look again at patterns of marriage which do not allow partners to become their true selves.

*10 September 1991*

Dear G.

You remember how, from time to time, we have discussed our single state. I have been trying to find words and images to describe how my own singleness 'feels', and how it is best made sense of. It seems to me that to believe in God does make it possible to derive a harvest from what could be seen only in terms of personal tragedy. It also seems that one can see it as some kind of useful sign to society – about what can be of unexpected value for our world, about the intrinsic value of the individual, about a challenge to the accepted ways of living which prevail in our different societies.

Your society is so obviously different from ours, but because you lived in England for nine years, you will understand mine better than I can understand yours. It would be good to pursue a few of the different issues which arise for each of us.

In our previous conversations, I sensed that you really are pioneering singleness for your own sisters in Zululand. Am I right in thinking all women were married until recently? If marriage was individually chosen, how did Zulu society bring about the marriage of men and women who had not naturally found themselves a partner? Was it through polygamy, or by some kind of arranged marriage? I imagine that the coming of the missionaries had a profound effect on local marriage patterns, so that monogamy replaced polygamy, but I don't understand why the phenomenon of single women has taken so long to appear.

I know your family has thrust upon you the care of your unmarried niece and her two children. I imagine this makes your place in society easier to understand, both for you and for others, but I suspect that you still feel uncertain in the world of couples. It may be that the African extended family makes things easier for you.

I should be interested to know how you see your life as a single woman in terms of your faith in God. Either one can feel that life has been less than kind, or else one can see singleness as some kind of gift, none too welcome at first, but gradually one which reveals its value for us and for those whom we try to serve. Someone has said that single-ness, and consequently celibacy, must be gifts, because they are so contrary to what is 'normal' for most of creation. In a society where the dominant minority white 'rulers' have ensured the break-up of traditional marriage patterns, your role as a single woman must be of particular significance in terms of an empowerment model for women left in the homelands, with all the responsibilities of the children, the home, and the creation of stability.

Some of that seems to come through in *Call Me Woman* (Kuzwayo, 1985). I wonder if that is how if feels to you? In a totally different situation here, but where traditional marriage patterns are changing radically, I feel in a con-tinuum of single women, certainly from the sixteenth cen-tury, who challenge society to see the value and ability of the single person, and refuse to allow them to see women (particularly) as appendages.

I hope you will write at some length and put right my inadequate understanding of what singleness means to you. I am hoping to write to B., and ask her the same kind of questions, as a single Indian Christian who has positively decided not to accept an arranged marriage.

Yours,
Margaret

*30 September 1991*

DEAR MARGARET

I have just received your fascinating letter. You have asked very thought-provoking questions, though some of the issues we have briefly discussed in the past. As you know, I am very busy and even busier now with the nurturing of our National Association for Women Empowerment (NAWE). However, sometimes I wonder if my taking on so many tasks is not a symptom of my own inner feelings about singleness, or an escape mechanism from reality.

I quite often say that living outside my own culture, or,

to be more specific, living in a Western culture, was the best thing that ever happened to me. According to Zulu culture, singleness is not accepted – for a man or for a woman. Women at a certain age of their lives will invariably attach themselves to any eligible bachelor, irrespective of match, of class or economic status. They just have to escape from many questions and remarks like, 'Have you not met anybody yet?' I have seen many women enter into very unhappy marriages because of this. In the past, many led very miserable lives, but now many divorce as the latter has become more tolerated. Looking back on my own life, I remember having an affair or two with men I now realize I was not really in love with, people with whom I had absolutely nothing in common. If I had got married, I either would have been very miserable or the marriage would have ended in divorce.

One of the things for which I am very grateful to my God is living in the UK for such a long time, as it changed my thinking completely. It took me completely outside my own culture, which was not always an advantage; you must ask me about readjusting to my culture, which was very traumatic. I learnt to accept myself for what I am; I learnt that I could live a normal life as a single woman. Many friends, you included, taught me how to live on my own and enjoy my own company. When I was on the Continent I met many still who were not that bothered about being single. Some cohabited, and did not contemplate marriage. In my own culture, I would have felt that I had been a failure. But not now – it does not even enter into my mind that anybody could think I am a failure. In fact, each time anyone talks about marriage to me, I take it as a joke.

What I can say is that during the times when life was a bit difficult I sometimes, though not often, wondered if it was not a blessing to have someone close in cases when one has to make important decisions, or to share grief. However, I soon discovered that a close person does not necessarily have to be a spouse. There are so many people who are lonely or lead single lives even though they are married to someone.

I also learnt while living in your culture that you are a

human being first and foremost. God created each one of us in his own image and each one has his/her special relationship with God: that relationship is much more special than any other. I also came to a conclusion, rightly or wrongly, that God shaped each individual's life the day they were born, and this shape cannot be easily tampered with.

However, being South African changes things a bit. One of the aftermaths of apartheid is the extremely high divorce rate among Blacks as well as Whites, though for different reasons. Of all women with whom I grew up, no fewer than seventy-five percent of those who married are now divorced. Even last week I saw somebody whom I had not seen since we were in nursing training together; she is bringing up her three children alone, having been divorced eight years ago. She tells such incredible tales of thirteen long years of misery, and a very nasty end to her marriage, her belongings thrown into the street while she was at work. That reinforced my current feeling of freedom, comfort, and no unhappy memories.

Having said that, I must also add that I am extremely fortunate to be educated and to come from the kind of family background as ours. I have a good job that includes very interesting research. The kind of education that I have had has also added another dimension to my current thinking: doing a study of attitudes to contraception, I have had to go deep into marriage in Zulu culture and have arrived at the conclusion that for a Zulu, being single has a lot of advantages.

Most women as they get older get desperate for children as well, but I never ever got that far. Friends put the idea into me by remarking that I am so good with kids, it is a pity I have not even adopted. But, as you know, God had his mysterious plans for me; I never thought that I would suddenly find myself raising two children. When my sister got married and my father died, I found myself lumbered with my sister's illegitimate daughter, who had spent three years at a reformatory and was most incorrigible. She fell pregnant, and I thought I was going to explode. I could not see a baby from our family growing in a terrible environment. I took the baby and sent my niece back to school.

Now she has two children, both of whom call me 'Ma'. They do not regard her as their mother at all, in spite of the fact that I am so often away from home. Now I could hardly live without them.

Being single still means loneliness in this culture, where people are not used to going out to concerts, eating out, etc. When there are parties, I never get invited – if I do I am included in my brother's invitation. People assume that I live with my brother and his family. As a jazz lover, I often drive to Durban on my own to a jazz concert. One of the main difficulties is when you think married people feel threatened and you feel you must retreat in most cases.

Keep well,
G.

*13 January 1992*

DEAR MARGARET

With continuing doubts about participating, I put pen to paper. My doubts stem from this being a personal matter – I do not speak for Asian women or Punjabi Christian women, but for myself. And this baring of souls is uncomfortable, although I have a good grasp of what the single life means to G., I do not feel I have a similar understanding of yours from your letter. Therefore, I am vague about what level of intimacy to pitch it.

However, here goes: being single means to me as the years progress, a growing inner strength, less flexibility in being able to compromise my own ideas, feelings, and actions. Being able to achieve without being held back in any sphere of life, particularly career.

Not being able to compromise does not mean stubbornness. It means being true to oneself. If I did not have this period of singleness and had detached myself from my father straight into another man, I don't know if I could have developed my own personality and ideas. I have been able to experience different ideas and make my own decisions. At times, it has been hard – sometimes I have been exposed to ideas contrary to the way I've been brought up as an Asian and Christian, or even as a member of the working class. I would not give any of these opportunities away or have my life back over to do things the expected or traditional way.

During the last few years, I have met some other single Asian women, as well as European white and Afro-Caribbean women. This has reduced my sense of isolation and helped fight off ideas that something is wrong with me for not desiring the concept of marriage and family at any cost.

It would seem natural for people who see the women's role mainly as a wife and mother to believe that a woman who does not want this, can not be 'natural'. However, I see it as perfectly natural to wait until one is ready both financially and emotionally for the great responsibility of having children. I am further cautious about marriage and children because of the consequences of bad marriages and poor parenting I see in my working life.

As G. said, the single life can be lonely at times: in social events, one does feel out on a limb. I have talked earlier about being responsible for myself and my own actions. However, my actions and thoughts are frequently still governed by how I was brought up, and sometimes this inhibits me. I still worry about the effects of my actions on family. Another consequence of being one's own person is that as you get older your standards get higher (or firmer), and the less likely it seems that you will meet anyone who meets them.

I'll end now, and as I do so, I am realizing I have made little comment on religion. I struggle with religion because I have yet to experience it as totally positive. I continue to see elements of it which are oppressive to various groups in society, including women. Perhaps resistance to see it another way comes from my background. I have very little experience of strong women in religion who have been able to argue against the ideas of men, women and marriage as preached by men (Asian men in my case).

Yours,
B.

*21 January 1992*

DEAR G.

I think all three of us would identify with B.'s experience of gaining an inner strength, and 'a being true to oneself'. Critics would tell us, I suspect, that this can be, and is, also gained in marriage and that only in the relationship of marriage can we be formed by love of another. I think we all need to wrestle in our second letter with whether as single people we are somehow less fully matured than our married sisters.

I think I personally would have to say that singleness has to be seen as a gift, just as marriage has to be, and that in whatever state of life we are called to live, we cannot evade the overriding obligation to become who we are. As I see it, each of us is saying in different ways that as we learn to live singly, we perceive ourselves enabled to take to ourselves more and more of our true selves. Would you say that was your experience? Does it seem easier or more difficult for you than for your married friends?

I think my observation is that many married women are not faced with this imperative until the children have grown up or until they lose their partner. Maybe we have the chance to grow into ourselves sooner? Anyway, it does seem disastrous to demand of life that it provides one with the ideal husband, and to turn away from the need to take responsibility for oneself. I like the way B. speaks of 'not desiring marriage or family at any cost'!

There is then the issue of what is 'natural'. B. points out that in common parlance, single people 'cannot be natural'. I think you can only say this if your definition of natural depends primarily on emphasizing the sexual side of marriage, both in itself and as resulting in having children and bringing them up. For B. and me, though not for you, we have a lot in common with infertile women. Society would say that at least they are married and in a sexual relationship.

I think I would want the prime vocation for anyone 'to become who they are' – to develop fully to the absolute limit of the gifts God has given them. Marriage and/or sexual relationships seem to me to be of less ultimate importance. As Christians, we have the example of Jesus doing the will of his Father, and really it is only in the Christian world that singleness has been seen as a viable option for men and women. I do not think Islam, Hinduism, or Sikhism give this same understanding to the idea that singleness can be a vocation. What do you see, within Christian society among your people?   .

Both you and B. support your own caution about getting married because of all the bad marriages you know about and all the harm done to children. Maybe we should see ourselves as having a positive message for our contemporaries, something like: 'It is all right to be single; more than that, it is *right* to be single rather than to hurry into marriage for the sake of being married, and so to debase the whole notion of marriage as a lifelong relationship.'

I also think we have to say something about religion as being oppressive to single people. I am sure that it is true, and that there is a general assumption in churches that the 'normal' unit is the family unit. But I would want to say that this arises from the Church taking on the ideas of the world, and not being true to Jesus's original message. I think his words about 'Whoever does the will of God is my brother and sister and mother' mean that the Christian family is different from the natural family, and does not rely on human ties, but on loyalty to him. He also commends those who have left family behind to follow him. I would want to say that following him has to include as a high priority a coming into being of my true self. How does that sound to you?   ,

I shall be fascinated to hear your answers. What do you think is the future for singleness among your people? Do say a bit about that.

With love,
Margaret

*1 February 1992*

DEAR MARGARET

I think there are interesting differences between B.'s experiences and mine. The main contributor to these is age. In a way it must be harder for her because she is young, whereas I have 'hardened', so to say, and also learnt to be content: in other words, have come to terms with being single, though I do not remember a time when I was terribly depressed by being single.

On the one hand, B. is lucky to be part of a society which has such a high population of single women that everybody has come to accept singleness. As a Zulu woman life is not always easy. Our Zulu culture emphasizes subordination of women; if fact, it is perpetuating itself very nicely, as women seem to enjoy being inferior to men. I had always boasted of being assertive, but I now realize that my being single is an additional handicap. I am currently having a house built. The architect and my brother often have meetings and do not invite me, the owner of the house. They make alterations to the plan without consulting me, let alone asking for my permission. Even my earnings I often have to share with the family at large. Had I not been single they would not dare, for my husband would not allow it. According to the Zulu tradition, the man that a daughter marries is given a very high status by his in-laws, irrespective of his social standing in society. I suppose through the husband the woman gains status, and with status comes respectability in our society. This is partly the reason why being married is so important.

When people meet me they ask, not if I am married, but 'To which clan are you married?' To say you are not married meets with a response of great amazement, disappointment, and even embarrassment. Therefore, being single means to rise above all these. I tell myself that my life is very full even if I am single. My relationship with God is very special and free. Whatever I am able to do to help others I do with ease as I am free – there is no other being who can come between me and God. In my case, singleness is a vocation. My house is full right now, in spite of the fact that I have borne no children biologically; that might not have been possible had I been married. There is also a lot of happiness and freedom in my house because it is an all-woman house.

I tell myself that God must not have wanted me to be married; if he had meant me to be married, he would have made a sexual relationship an important issue in my life. We are all different. Some people need more food than others; some people need emotional support more than others. I feel I do not need that support necessarily from a sexual relationship. To put it differently, there is more to a relationship than the sexual side.

Religion is not oppressive to single people, I think; rather the Church. The Church insists on marriage and the 'natural family unit', but God created each one of us as individuals in this true image, but not the family.

Among my people education will bring freedom. Single people are beginning to hold positions in the Church; they are only now beginning to say 'Yes, I am single, so what?' Also very high is the divorce rate among professional women; not that I applaud this. What it implies is that they are not prepared to be men's slaves. They are beginning to take a stand; they are exercising their right to question and their right to choose. Pity our education standards have been allowed to decline. We already have a semi-literate generation. In as far as this issue is concerned, we are going to have to progress quite a bit before the situation improves.

G.

*18 February 1992*

DEAR B.

I have today had a response from G. to your last letter, which I enclose. The main theme to emerge seems to be the positive value of being single as a challenge to norms of society and of the Church.

G. is clearly seeing her singleness as a challenge to other

single people to dare to be free of enslaving patterns of marriage and as a challenge to the assumption that everyone has to have a sexual relationship to be fulfilled. I think she also sees her sense of singleness as a vocation, as a challenge to the Church and its insistence on the 'natural family unit'.

I suppose I had seen this before in my own life, but G. has helped me to see it more clearly and to be able to articulate what I have felt instinctively. Not that this makes it an easy state of life, but it gives it purpose, especially in terms of liberation for others.

I would not want to suggest that I am against marriage, on the contrary, but if my own striving to live as a single person in the most creative and contented way that I can, helps other people to dare to think that being who they are is a vitally important part of life, and that it can enable more fulfilling marriages for both partners, then I am happy.

I would like you to respond on this theme, I think. Can you, or do you, see your own struggle not to submit to an arranged marriage, and somehow to have to live singly until, or if, you get married as something which is not only for your own integrity, but also for the good of your own community?

It would also be good, if you felt able to look at the issue of celibacy – not having to submit to the almost universal assumption that sexual relationships are vital for everyone. I would want to say that myself, though I do not find it easy, but then I don't observe marriage relationships to be easy either.

And lastly, the Church. I like G.'s ability to distinguish between her free relationship to God, and not to see that as in any way oppressive, and her differentiation between religion and the Church. I do think the male clergy and many of the laity talk and act as though only married people actually exist. I feel we need to work to upgrade the value and dignity of single people, especially of single women, within the Church. I guess your experience is probably much more destructive than mine, and you may need to be more angry and more outspoken to the Church – and even to God?

Thank you so much for helping.

Love,
Margaret

*6 March 1992*

DEAR MARGARET

A quick reply to yours and G.'s letters. Firstly, let me say single life does not necessarily 'depress' me. What depresses me is that society makes it difficult for single people – maybe women in particular – i.e. going out, assumptions about marriage and children being the vocation of all women. Being single only hits home at certain times and situations. Most of the time I find single life quite enjoyable, and actually think it's an easy option. There's too many problems and compromises in a relationship – especially marriage.

This period of singleness was a necessity for me for personal growth. It was not a decision about/against marriage *per se*, or sexual relationship or celibacy. My singleness isn't a statement to anyone but my family, myself, and perhaps to other women – especially Asian women. Being single has a perfectly valid status and is even an alternative to marriage. Women do not necessarily need men in order to be fulfilled or to survive, and children are not necessarily the vocation of women. But singleness was primarily for myself – not society or the Church.

It is often said that women do not have the same feelings about sex as men, i.e., whereas men want more sex, women want more love. Therefore, living a celibate life when there is not a loving relationship in existence does not present any great difficulties I think. However, I do not equate single life with celibacy, nor have any judgements regarding whether it is good to be celibate or have a sexual relationship. For me, the fight has been for the right to choose for oneself – one chooses to be celibate or have a sexual relationship – it's their choice. Of course, there's the usual guidelines about safe sex, etc.

41

I'm horrified that G. is still having problems with close relatives letting her make her own decisions, for example about her house. There's many correlations between the Zulu attitude towards women and the Asian perspective – but even though I have not made major changes in social attitudes, my brothers and father will no longer make any decisions – small or large – on my behalf. Neither will they talk for me to architects or salespersons when I'm having difficulties.

It is interesting that arranged marriages invariably crop up – perhaps because I'm Asian. But 'arranged' covers a whole spectrum of situations. It does not necessarily mean meeting your partner on your wedding day. My refusal to get married may have seemed on the surface a statement against marriages – but on hindsight, it was mainly about space to be myself and make choices for myself – concerning timing and alternatives. For me, there's no guarantee that European Christian marriages will be any more loving and equal than partnership of any other religion or culture.

Yours,
B.

REFERENCES

Kuzwayo, E. (1985). *Call Me Woman*. London, Women's Press.
Moore, S. (1980). *The Fire and the Rose Are One*. London, Darton, Longman and Todd.

# 4 *Mothercare*

ANN LEWIN

## *Mother and Child*

I wonder what you are thinking as you sit there.
Are you remembering how you washed the
Child you bore? These hands, so
Frail and gnarled now, washed and
Gentled me. Now I wash you.
Your feet, so painful sometimes,
Carried you on endless journeys of caring;
Kneeling to wash them is an act of homage.
Are you remembering how when you were young
You pleased yourself about what you wore, and
Where you went? Now another puts your clothes ready,
And guides your unsteady steps.
Who is the child now, who the mother?
Do you remember sitting as I do,
Torn between wanting to help, and needing to
Leave dignity and independence free? Was it
A kind of death to you, that to be free,
I had to grow away? Your freedom now
Can only come through death, a
Painful letting go for both of us.

We'll never talk about these things,
But sometimes, when I tuck you into bed,
You look at me with impish humour,
As though you know what I am thinking,
Child, mother.

## *Mother*

My brain, why won't it work?
When what's her name,
The person looking after me,
Asks what I'd like for tea,
The choices slither out of reach
And I don't know.
Dressing's another thing:
Those clothes, I used to
Put them on in seconds,
Now I can't remember how to do it,
And sometimes go downstairs
Without my dress. You'd think
I'd realize – I feel such a fool.
My memory – ask me what happened when
Scott reached Antarctica, and I can tell you
How I read about it to the school, best
Reader of them all. But ask me
What I've had for dinner, and
I can't remember. Have I had my dinner?

They take me out, that's good.
We watch the sea, and laugh at people
Falling off those boards;
Or go where there are animals, they know
I love to see the newborn ones.
I store up all my news to tell
Whoever hasn't taken me,
But when we meet, I can't remember,
And tell them anything to cover up
This muddle in my head.
But we all know it isn't right.
I've lived too long. They're very kind,
And say it isn't true. But really we all know.
'Ah, hello dear, I hoped you'd come.
I want to tell you – what was it?'

# Mothercare

## Daughter

Dear Mum, she gets so muddled,
Such a shame. She loses things –
We never found her teeth –
Or hides them. Was there a childhood
Prohibition about food being left on plates?
That would explain leftovers hidden
In the pot she puts her teeth in
When she's tired of wearing them.
A nice surprise for whoever cleans her teeth,
The new ones, that is. I hate false teeth,
And that pot. Neither will survive her long!
Those men who wake her early in the morning,
Clearing the snow (improbable in June)
Or pumping water, who are they? 'They're
Something at the college', she says
Knowingly. And all those crowds of people
Who go past at night, invisible to us –
'A special meeting somewhere, about
Something', – she always knows.
'What's today? Then where did Monday go?
Tomorrow I shall only have two pills.
I always know it's Wednesday by the pills.'
But tomorrow she'll say, 'Only two? Why's that?'

It's been a busy day, the gasman called,
Hardly disturbing the tedium of her time.
She who bore children, ran a home,
Rarely sat idle, can't remember that,
Looks blankly at a picture of her husband
Married to her more than fifty years.
Then mother's instinct surfaces,
She puts the kettle on for tea.

A burnt dry kettle has a special smell –
We always have a spare now, just in case.
At least the gas lit this time . . .
'I thought there was a funny smell,' she says.
Dear Mum.

# Women's Lives

## Still Growing

My mother died some time ago.
The person I now care for,
Though she looks the same,
Has lost her power.
No longer archetypal,
Giver of life, solver of problems,
Source of wisdom, but
A frail old lady, confused and
Almost past the stage of knowing it.
(Though suddenly the other night
She said, 'Old age defeats me,
Who'd have thought that I'd go
Funny in the head like this?')

Watching her tears me inwardly.
Why should she suffer this disintegration,
Going on wearily from day to day?

Yet in her waiting there is hope.
Delightful still in personality,
She grows serenely on to her next stage.
Faltering strength and ceasing to be mother
Are staging posts, not ends, for her.
She's waiting in anticipation for her next
Adventure. 'When the time is right,' she says,
'I'll go.'

### Identity Crisis

A nightied figure on the stairs
The second time that evening,
'I can't sleep.'
Once more I led my mother back to bed.
'Sleep well,' I said, 'I'll soon be up myself.'
'Don't disturb Ann', she said maternally.
'I won't', said Ann.

### Second Childhood

We sit and watch the sky change,
And she tells me how she used to sit
In childhood at the farm, and
Watch the sunset, glorious colours
Streaking the horizon.
And now a second childhood,
Cruel in reversal.
No growth to independence, as
One by one abilities are lost.
Sleep is not now renewal, only a
Respite from dulled sense and memory.
Frustration, once alleviated by
Mastery of skills, increases as the
Need for help grows greater, personal
Freedom less. Life goes full circle,
Death a second birth.

> *Grow old along with me,*
> *The best is yet to be...*
> Robert Browning

Undoubtedly, Browning's view of ageing is true for some, but for those to whom old age brings increasing frailty and disintegration, the picture is rather different. My mother lived for nearly thirteen years after my father's death. For the first two, she was relatively independent, living quite a normal life for a seventy-seven year old. Then, almost overnight, the picture changed. It became clear that she was not coping: she became confused, at first in little ways, then more seriously; her sense of time went; she forgot how to cook. Operation Mothercare began in earnest.

Mother had lived in the same house for over fifty years. One of my brothers lived with her, I lived just down the road; both of us unmarried, both in full-time work. Her local friends were mostly her age, and not in a position to help. I was fortunate in finding a young neighbour who wanted a part-time job. For the next five years, she spent most of the morning with mother, got her lunch, then left her to sleep until it was time to come back and get her tea. After that, my brother and I took over. Within a year, mother's condition was such that she qualified for the attendance allowance – she didn't need heavy nursing, but she wasn't safe on her own for any length of time. For the eleven or so years of Mothercare, she was never left alone in the house at night, or for very long during the day.

When that neighbour gave up, an even more elaborate system of care was devised. I was blessed with some very good friends who were willing to come and spend the day with Mum for very little financial reward. As they knew each other, two, later three, of them organized the care between them. The time between my brother going to work before 8 am, and the carer arriving after children had been dropped at school was my responsibility, as was the early part of the evening. I used to call in on my way to work and set up the day – check that mother was dressed properly, that there was enough food, and so on. After work, I would go back for a couple of hours, get a meal for myself and oversee mother's bedtime – she rarely wanted to stay up much after 6 pm – and generally hold the fort until my brother came home. In the winter months, he was usually there during the evening, in the summer, I took over when the cricket season occupied him. Weekends we shared, and when he went away, I moved in. If we both wanted to be out at the same time, I found a sitter.

An important part of the Mothercare, then, was management. Mostly it worked well, but there were times when the system fell apart. At one point, I found myself knocking at the doors of complete strangers where I knew there was a woman with small children, or not out at work, in an attempt to find a suitable carer to fit into the system. Care in the community can work, but let no one be deceived into thinking that it is cheap. Not much money changed hands, it's true: the attendance allowance is a pittance compared to what the carers should have been paid, and we had few other resources. I saved the authorities thousands of pounds by organizing mother's care, but only because I accepted the exploitation of my goodwill, and exploited others too. Harsh words, but the only accurate ones I can find.

Financial considerations are only part of the cost. I wrote quite a lot, descriptive of what was happening, during the last six years or so of mother's life, in the sequence of poems printed at the beginning of this chapter. They tell something of what it was like. The first big challenge came when I began to wash my mother. She hated it. I wasn't too keen myself, but it had to be done. Part of my reluctance came from realizing that this marked another stage in her loss of independence, but part from the fact that in our family nakedness was taboo. Early messages were very strong: my father's antics on the beach as he struggled to put on his far-from-revealing bathing trunks under the shelter of the largest towel we possessed, induced not only hastily suppressed mirth but also the belief that bodies were to be concealed. I broke the taboo with my father when I helped look after him during the last year of his life; caring for someone with a colostomy doesn't leave much room for modesty. But I had to overcome the reluctance again with my mother. It was even harder for my brother – right up to the time when she went into hospital, just over a year before she died, if she thought my brother was approaching she would call out to warn him if she was not 'decent'. And he had to call for female assistance if any intimate care was needed. In many ways, the physical care of others is easier for a woman, I suppose because nursing skills have traditionally been seen as belonging to the area of woman's work. But the fact that it is often women who care should not blind us to the needs of men who look after others.

As mother's ability to amuse herself diminished, she became reliant on us to entertain her. She loved going for a car ride, and on any day when my brother or I were there, as soon as dinner was over – sometimes before we had finished – she would disappear upstairs and get her hat and coat. Whether we wanted to or not, one of us took her for a ride. She seldom remembered where she'd been, but she loved being out in the country or by the sea. We covered hundreds of miles over the years, pointing out interesting things to her. We still sometimes surprise our passengers by drawing attention to lambs or blossom which they can perfectly well see for themselves – it has become as automatic as driving. Once we'd persuaded her to use a wheelchair, it was easier; we could visit stately homes or gardens instead of driving ever onward. But we learnt to treat the information that places were accessible to wheelchairs with caution – some must have been designated by people who'd never pushed an occupied chair uphill, or over tree-roots, or tried to restrain one as it went rather too fast downhill.

The people who cared for mother loved coming. One of the many blessings was that her dementia didn't make her aggressive. She would doze and chat alternately, keeping her carers amused with tales of her youth on the farm. She wasn't quite so reliable about contemporary affairs though, and her desire to make it appear that she was still in control led her to make up what she didn't know, sometimes with confusing results. But even though she was lovely, the demands of care were unrelenting. It was like having a baby who would never grow up, who would in fact become more dependent. Eight years into the care, I wrote 'De Profundis'.

> How long. O lord, how long?
> A silly question.
>
> Do you, beyond the tick of time,
> For whom a thousand years
> Flash like an evening,
> Do you know how it feels
> When evenings, days, months,
> Drag, a thousand years?
> The seeming endlessness of care,
> Commitment carrying on
> Long after energy is spent,
> Do you, who slumber not,
> Know that bone-weariness?
>
> 'My strength sufficient.' Yes,
> I hear you, Lord. My head
> Acknowledges that you are right.
> The question in my guts is,
> Is it true? Can I hang on
> Until your timelessness
> Pervades my life, and
> Makes the question meaningless?

Perhaps it was as well that I didn't know at that stage there were still more than two years to go.

Giving physical care was the easiest part of cradling my mother in love. Reassuring her during the period of her mental deterioration drew deeply on my resources. The years when she was aware of 'going funny' were hard. 'I'm a silly old woman', she would say. 'Not silly, just old', I would reply. But I don't think I convinced her. The indignity of becoming incontinent caused her great distress – I was relieved when she became so out of touch mentally that she didn't seem to notice. It's hard to watch someone you love deteriorate. Caring tears you apart, as you go on helping them to live even when you believe it's more than time they died. There are times when life is held by such a thin, trembling thread that it would be easy to snap it. I prayed that my mother would die – her freedom, and ours, would only come through death. When her life was prolonged by the quality of care she was given, I wondered if God felt as frustrated as I did. I was aware that the agony was shared by the professionals too: it's hard for doctors and nurses to judge the moment for ceasing to try too hard to prolong life. All I could do was make it plain that as far as the family was concerned, at the point they felt it was medically appropriate, they should feel free to cease to treat my mother. I hoped they would reach that point sooner rather than later.

For some, the strain becomes too much. Just round the corner, a woman we knew quite well was murdered by her son. People were shocked and saddened, but some understood better than others. His concern apparently had been that he was going to die before her, and he couldn't see how she would be cared for. More recently, I was very moved to hear a friend describe how she had decided that she would have to kill her father, because she couldn't bear the way he had been reduced to helplessness by his infirmity. Mercifully, people realized how near to breaking-point she was, and came to her rescue in time. Some people are driven to ill treatment of the old or ill, just as they are with babies: few, I imagine, escape thoughts that are hard to admit to because they are so shocking. But for the grace of God, a lot of us would be in trouble.

I have written so far about physical and emotional needs: there were her spiritual needs too. Mum always used to listen to the daily service on the radio, and sing along with the hymns. When she became too frail to go to church, TV services (as long as they were familiar in style) became her spiritual nourishment, along with Communion, which the local vicar brought her every month. Eventually, her ability to recognize what was going on diminished beyond the point of being able to cope with abstract things like radio waves. It was about that time that I began to sing to her as I put her to bed. She'd had a lovely voice in her day, and used to sing around the house – in fact the family used to sing together quite often when we were all at home. For the last eighteen months of her life, I sang to her most nights, even in hospital. I was rather taken aback one night to find the rest of the ward listening too. Mum loved being sung to, and her face lit up at some of the familiar tunes from her childhood. Some of the evening hymns are very good prayers, especially as death draws near.

Religion was a subject that we didn't discuss in our family, though it was important to us. Occasionally, when she was still able to be rational, the fact of her impending death would surface as we chatted at bedtime, and we talked about it a bit. I knew she was not afraid to die, and in some ways welcomed the prospect of release from the constraints of her frailty and looked forward to meeting again those who'd already had the adventure. As life became more bewildering for her, the hymns I sang became my way of praying with her – it was important to keep reminding her that she was held in God's love, however strange her experience of losing touch.

Fifteen months before she died, mother was admitted into hospital with a chest infection, and not for the first time, we prepared ourselves to say goodbye. Her generation was a tough one though, and she survived. She was discharged into a rest home, where she was cared for extremely well during her long decline. We were spared agonizing decisions about whether to put her into a home or not – there was no choice. We couldn't provide the kind of care she needed at home, nor could we talk to her about it – by this time she didn't know where she was or who we were. But she was still our concern, and this last stretch was harder emotionally in many ways than the years before. Then we had been kept busy by a very tight schedule, now there was time to spend with her, but little chance of relating to her as a person. I had said many goodbyes over the years; waiting for the last one, experiencing a kind of arrested bereavement, was very painful. Another poem, 'Farewells', written during this period, explored the experience:

I always hated those times at the station,
When, goodbyes said, we found ourselves
Locked into meaningless chatter or
Awkward silences, as the train
Waited for its signal.
What could we say? No conversation
Could be guaranteed completion.
Pain of parting
Smarted behind the eyelids
As we struggled to be cheerful.

Waiting as life draws to its close
Can be like that. Longing for release,
But dreading the moment of departure.

The waiting seemed endless; and the last poem I wrote about
the experience of those last months, after she had died,
describes it, and the mixture of emotions I felt at her death:

I visited each day
To see if she was there;
To catch a flicker of response,
A smile. But she was gone,
Lingering in another place
Until her unresponsive body
Could catch up with dying.
A winter of waiting, then
Just at the greening of the spring,
Released, she died.

I do not weep for her,
Born to new life;
The tears I shed are for myself,
An adult who has lost a friend,
A child her mother.

Those years were lived in the context of believing in God
and trying to be faithful. In my experience, believing in God
doesn't solve any problems, especially when you are wrestling with impossible situations. What it does do is offer a
new set of resources. I knew myself to be held in a love

which was greater than anything else, even when it didn't 'put things right'. But that knowledge didn't make things easier, nor had it been gained in any facile way. It was a knowledge won through many experiences when my life had threatened to fall apart, when, struggling to hang on to the promise of God's faithfulness, I'd found, incredibly, sufficient indications of his care to go on trusting. This was another such time, when the questions were sharpened up again.

When my mother, aged ninety, was struggling to die, as I walked to work one day, a man in his fifties dropped dead just in front of me, leaving a widow, and two sons at university. Cruel irony. 'You must be left with some questions', said a friend when I told him about it. True, but in the end, it was only one: 'Does God know what he's doing?' I don't believe God sends suffering, as a test or for any other reason. Given the situation, I desperately wanted him to intervene and put things right for my mother. (It was too late for the widow and her sons.) But that raised another problem, because I don't believe in that sort of God either. He has given the universe laws which it has to follow, and there was no reason why they should be varied for me or my mother. I did not doubt that God was in it all somewhere, the question was, where? And as I railed at the delay which was causing so much pain, feeling the birthpangs of my mother's death, I came to fresh understanding. A God who makes people suffer, or who acts capriciously, would not be a God worth worshipping, but a God who has made himself vulnerable by offering us responsibility (free will, in theological jargon) who suffers with us and is brought to his knees with us (isn't that what the Incarnation is about?), and who continually brings new life out of dead ends, that is a God I can relate to. Not obviously omnipotent, but skilled in crisis management (or learning fast). He and I can exchange a few wry smiles about that.

We've had a few wry exchanges too over what I sometimes refer to as the design fault in the female of species. A woman's lifecycle has several points of change: I became acutely aware, as one of them bore heavily upon me, that the menopausal years are those when women are most likely to be called on to cope with adolescents struggling to find their own sense of meaning and value, and with elderly parents losing theirs. Not the best timing in the world. In my case the adolescent young were not mine – a fact which had its own pain, as I came to fresh realization of my own childlessness. When I parted company with teaching through early retirement, (yet another facet of midlife crisis) at least I was spared the menopausal/adolescent conflicts, but I still didn't have the freedom that might have been helpful to deal with my own growing pains. Women at many stages of their lives are simply not able to indulge in the luxury of being ill, and many who might, during the menopausal years, have benefited from a hysterectomy or lesser surgery, have not been able to take advantage of it because the demands of care are too great. I can rejoice with the Psalmist when he says of the human body, 'I am fearfully and wonderfully made', but there have been many times when I've said the words through gritted teeth.

What kept me sane through those years of caring was being able to live a 'normal' life – though that also contributed to the exhaustion. I had learnt in my late teens, when I had done another lesser stint of mothercare, that friendships don't always survive a period of non-availability. When I entered into this commitment I was very clear that I was not going to sacrifice myself on any altar of filial devotion. But I could only live that 'normal' life with a lot of help, from the brother who shared the care, and the many friends who gave us both freedom. When I gave up full-time work and took a part-time job, I deliberately kept the Monday-Friday care pattern in operation, so that I had time for myself. Apart from ensuring that re-entry into ordinary pursuits would be possible, it made me a more interesting, fulfilled person, with more to offer to the care, bringing news from the outside world into the very confined life my mother had to lead. There are many support groups now for home-carers, but the last thing I wanted was a self-help group. When I was up to the limit with caring, I had little desire to go and swop stories with other people.

Being patient with mother's frustrations was easier than being patient with my own. In the face of bureaucracy I was sometimes reduced to impotent fury – it seemed that the more you were seen to be coping, the more you would be required to do. My attempt to get help with washing my mother is a case in point. I used to give her a good wash once a week – that was fine at first, but became more difficult as she deteriorated. In the evening she was too tired; it was no good telling her to wait for me in the morning (she forgot, or moved the note I left on her clothes to remind her), and I hadn't the heart to make her undress again if she'd got her clothes on in the right order. If she hadn't, I sometimes slipped in a quick wash. It got harder and harder to maintain a weekly pattern, and I felt things could be better. The nurse who came to assess the situation asked me what the problem was: 'There are many in worse case', she said. No doubt true, but that didn't help me, either to feel better about what I thought was a failure to care properly for my mother's bodily needs, or actually to improve the care.

I won't start on the problems with the DSS over income support payments when mother eventually went into the rest home – the long delay before payments began (they lost the papers), demands for the payment book to be sent back for adjustment and not returned for a fortnight or more; 'forgetting' to notify us of an increase in the rate due; the fact that income support always leaves you short of what is required for fees (and it's worse for people in nursing homes). My blood pressure was raised more than a little – and I know that I am not alone in these experiences.

From my experience, as well as from observation, I would say that there are a number of things carers need to support them, and churches could develop some strategies to assist. First and foremost, carers need adequate help, both in terms of physical provision and in terms of finance. Carers have to do two things: love the person and give the care. Sometimes the demands of the latter affect the quality of the former. People need help to discern what it is appropriate to do in terms of residential care. The words, 'putting someone in a home' are highly emotive, and can awaken terrible guilt feelings in those who have to decide. When the relationship has been good, it's hard; when the relationship has been poor, it's hell. Some people are driven to go on trying to provide the care long after the point when they should have given up; and families, where not all the members take an equal share of responsibility, are not always of one mind about what is right.

Carers need real opportunities to lead a normal life and keep outside interests and relationships going, so that in the end, return to mainstream living is possible. I don't want to minimize the value of self-help groups, only to encourage imagination in the provision of other kinds of freedom too.

Those involved in care need to be taken seriously, and listened to as they struggle with their own emotions, doubts, fears and murderous thoughts. They need the encouragement of being recognized as people who are indeed doing a grand job, but in a way that doesn't make them feel guilty because they know inside that they are not as marvellous as all that.

They need help in struggling with belief in God, when it is by no means clear who God is, or whether s/he is in control; help in staying with the questions, not the provision of answers which deny the questions' validity.

Carers need to know that there is a political will to bring about change, to know that there are people working for justice in the provision of care for the old and sick which does not exploit either the clients or the carers.

And then, when the time of care is over, they need support and understanding as they live with a sense of loss which is no less great because it was anticipated and in some sense longed for; as they adjust to a life where what has been a main reason for their existence is no longer there; and as they move into and through the hard work of grieving.

NOTE

Ann Lewin's poems are available from the author at 17 Sirdar Road, Portswood, Southampton SO2 3SH. Her latest collection is entitled *Candles and Kingfishers*, £2.50. Please add 25% for post and packing.

# 5  *Seeing Ourselves in a New Light*
## FAITH O'REILLY

Our sexuality is our desire to participate in making love, making justice in our world; our drive towards one another; our movement in love; our expression of being bonded together in life and death. Sexuality is expressed not only between lovers in personal relationships, but also in the work of an artist who loves her painting and poetry, a father who loves his children, a revolutionary who loves her people. (Heyward, 1984)

*In this interview with a professional artist, we explore how the links between sexuality and spirituality have affected her life, her relationships, and her creativity.*

**Q:** Some people would argue that there are links between sexuality and artistic creativity. I wonder if you could explore with us how that has been true in your life.

**A:** I suspect that many children who have a creative talent often become quite solitary, because they recognize that in some ways they are different. I don't want to over-generalize from my experience, but I can recall that as a child I separated myself from others in order to develop my drawing and painting. At the time I was also a fairly devout Catholic, and I felt that if I had a talent, which was given to me by God, I wanted to develop it both for myself and in order to help others to find theirs too.

One of the consequences of this was that I did not participate much in many of the 'normal' adolescent experiences of sexual experiment. I probably identified more with boys that with girls in terms of gender stereotypes, and it was only in my late adolescence that I realized I was lesbian. In those days – thirty years ago – the word was hardly mentioned in social circles, and so there were very few people to whom I could turn and talk about my sexuality. That, too, was a very isolating experience.

I was extraordinarily lucky because my parents moved to the same village as the artist Stanley Spencer. He gave me enormous help and support in developing my artwork, and we spent a lot of time together. At the time I was painting quite a number of religious pictures of biblical scenes: for example the feeding of the five thousand, and the Last Supper. One was donated to a local Roman Catholic church, and as far as I know is still there.

One of the pictures I painted was of Christ holding the host. It's one which presents Jesus as a fairly androgynous figure: beyond the categories of male and female. At the same time, I wanted to portray Christ as a human being so I ensured that his features were those of an Israeli. All too often portrayals of him seemed to me to be those of a White, Aryan male figure, so I wanted to offer another artistic interpretation.

At the same time as I was painting religious pictures, I wondered if I was losing my faith. I went initially to talk to a priest, and I recall him encouraging me to keep painting the pictures and also to keep coming to church. And of course I recognized that although Stanley Spencer was a religious artist of considerable stature, he too had conflicts in making links between his faith, his sexuality, and his art. So in a way I had two 'authority figures' to turn to in late adolescence, who both in different ways affirmed me in developing my creativity and spirituality.

However, I had also begun a relationship with a woman. This was very important to me in my sexual development, and gave me an enormous sense of personal liberation; but when I contemplated talking about my sexuality with a priest, I felt I had to go to confession, which was a less personal encounter. At the time I would have expressed my thoughts as 'impure', and was indeed told not to see the woman concerned again, which of course was really quite devastating.

**Q:** In that sense it sounds as if there were a lot of contradictions for you to hold together: on the one hand a strong religious belief which was changing, and on the other a lack of acceptance of your sexual orientation by a representative of the institutional church.

**A:** Yes – I suppose it was a very painful time for me, and one which was associated with a lot of confusion. It was not just about attitudes of the Church: it was also true in the difficulties of finding support anywhere. Interestingly, again I confided in two men about my sexuality, and found that quite a damaging experience too. One of the men concerned went mad, and I mean mad. He did his best to break up the relationship. He told my landlady, who also said that I couldn't have my friend to stay any more. He managed to break into the box where I kept my letters from her, and robbed me of them. He also wrote to my girl-friend's father, who was not best pleased either.

Looking back, I suspect that the man who did these things was sexually jealous, and his anger was a product of that. However, the effect on me was to make me feel dirty, guilty, and rejected. It was a time when I went back into my shell and found little support from anyone at all, least of all in a village which was fairly upper-middle-class, and respectably married. In fact, I was almost drummed out of the village when word got round that I was involved in a relationship with a woman.

**Q:** In that series of isolating and distressing experiences, with little or no support, how did you survive?

**A:** Well, I suppose I felt very fragile – and felt initially as if I had to prove I was not lesbian, mainly to satisfy social convention. I did develop a relationship with a man, and it lasted some time, but of course it was not fulfilling for either of us. So in the end it fizzled out.

At about the same time, Stanley Spencer died, which meant I lost one of my chief sources of support and inspiration. I hung around the village for a little while, and then went on to teaching, and studied at the Royal Academy in London. Inevitably, the subject-matter of my paintings altered as my environment and influences also changed; but I still explored some Christian themes in my painting.

One of the things I wanted to paint was the Assumption, but this proved to be extraordinarily difficult. For me, my Catholic background and the centrality of Mariology offers a potential sense of symmetry, between the Ascension and the Assumption, the male god figure and the female goddess figure if you like, and each being taken up to heaven. But the problem with portraying such events, which are much more mystical and symbolic, and quite foreign to our twentieth-century mind, is that it is very hard to encapsulate them visually. They are part of a much more imaginative world-view, which can be dismissed as irrational. In artistic terms, the obvious framework for exploring them would be that of the Surrealists, whose work portrayed the world of dreams, mythology, and the unconscious in the earlier part of this century. I suppose for me it was impossible to convey awe, wonder, and mystery sufficiently. Perhaps there are dimensions of religious experience which can't be visualized in that kind of way, and are better conveyed through words or music. I suspect I'd find that was also true for me of the Resurrection.

I now live in a permanent relationship with my current partner. We met over twenty years ago, and although I recognize that our experience is not typical of all lesbian couples, our relationship has had a profound and deep effect on me. I recall, however, that when we met I was afraid of even suggesting we might have a sexual relationship for fear of losing the friendship, so it took quite a long time for us to recognize and acknowledge the reality of what was going on. Living in a culture which denies and devalues lesbian relationships, and having been quite painfully punished for my sexuality, it was unlikely that either of us would be in a hurry to start a sexual relationship.

Although lesbian relationships at the time weren't subject to legal constraint, relationships between men were still illegal. So the whole area of same-sex relationships was far less acceptable than it is today. I'm not therefore saying that all is well for lesbian and gay people, but the whole cultural climate about sexuality is different. Certainly in the last ten years I have noticed that sexuality is discussed far more openly, for example by the students I taught, than it ever was when I was an equivalent age. And that seems very open and positive to me.

It would be difficult to comment on the development of my art during that period of change, because I was teaching others rather than doing my own work as I am now. However, one interesting side-effect of some of the teaching I did was that several people who came to the art class I ran were suffering quite a lot of psychological distress for one reason or another. I wouldn't want to suggest I was offering something which was professional art therapy, because that is a specialist area in itself, and I wasn't qualified to work in that way. I did find, though, that sometimes the work I did overlapped with others who were working in the areas of professional counselling. It was sometimes helpful to see how our areas of work were complementary; certainly that was true with one of the local chaplains in higher education, who was counselling someone who attended my classes.

Q: Have your own religious beliefs become less institutionalized – or would you still retain a connection with the Catholic Church?

A: Well, I suspect I spent quite a long time in the wilderness after my experience of confession; after all, people are unlikely to go to church if they feel their sexual orientation is unacceptable to the institution. I know how much negativity some members of the lesbian and gay community feel towards the Church, and how many of them are ex-Christians. I don't know if that is statistically significant or not, but I wonder if it has something to do with the ways that people absorb messages about the repression of their sexuality from the institution.

However, I began to realize that I didn't want to exclude myself from a faith which has meant so much to me. I'd also met a number of people who were also Christian, so I decided to return to the Church. I do have to say that my first attempt to go to Mass was rather disastrous. It was at the time of one of the abortion debates in Parliament, and when we came to the sermon, almost the first words were, 'Murderers, you are all murderers..!' I remember looking round at the rest of the congregation, who seemed just about as baffled and astonished as I was. I have to say that after that incident it took me some time to dare to set foot in a church again, but now I go quite regularly to Mass. I enjoy the symbolism, the sense of awe and mystery, and the ways it speaks to me of transcendence.

Q: It seems from what you are saying that you have needed to challenge prejudice and misunderstanding in order to find yourself spiritually, personally, and professionally. Is this something you still work at consciously today?

A: Well it's hard to say, because a lot has depended on where I've lived and what job I've been doing. I suspect that I've been in a position professionally where people have drawn their own conclusions about my sexual orientation, so I haven't been very explicit about it. Given that communication is non-verbal as well as verbal, I'm fairly sure that people pick up coded visual messages: for example, I don't dress to attract men in the way that some women might. But I also recognize that I'm not as overtly political about my sexuality as some members of the lesbian community are; though I suspect that's to do with my generation.

I wonder if I had been more up-front about my sexuality, whether I would have had a harder time. Prejudices about lesbian women operate in all sorts of odd ways: for example, whether or not we are likely to have sexual relationships with students. But that is surely going to be as true of heterosexual people as of lesbian and gay people.

Socially, one of the things which my partner and I notice is that when some heterosexual couples come to a meal they don't quite know how to relate to us, partly because of gender stereotyping. Even if I do the cooking they may assume I'm the 'man' in the partnership; and yet the reality of our relationship – as of any sexual relationship – is that it is a complex and subtle interaction in terms of qualities of personality. The butch/femme stereotyping which some used to associate with lesbian relationships is not by any means universally adopted nowadays.

I've just taken early retirement, which has enabled me to devote myself more full-time to my painting. This has enabled me to spend part of the time painting in France. I suppose in terms of content my work is now less explicitly religious, although the activity of painting is one which some regard as spiritual, since it requires a similar level of consciousness as prayer or meditation.

One aspect of working in France is that of the quality of the light: something which the Impressionists often talked about, but I had to experience for myself. In our house there is one painting of new light dawning, which has always seemed to me to be an expression of where my spirituality is at the moment. Perhaps it is symbolic of the possibility of new beginnings in all sorts of aspects of human existence.

REFERENCE

Heyward, C. (1984). *Our Passion for Justice*. New York, Pilgrim Press.

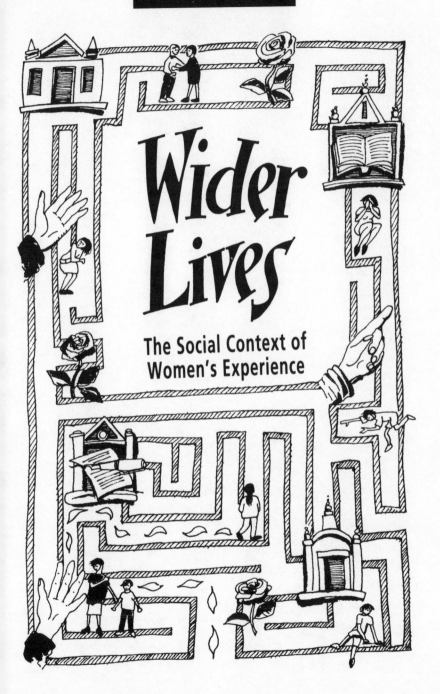

# PART TWO

# Wider Lives

## The Social Context of Women's Experience

In this section, contributors speak from various perspectives within culture, society, and public policy about the structural and institutional factors which shape women's experiences and needs.

Alison Peacock, writing about adult education for women, argues that standards of attainment for women often reinforce stereotypical models of vocation and aptitude. She illustrates how inappropriate understandings of women's caring may preclude them from realizing their full intellectual potential.

Hazel Addy explores a pattern of pastoral care relevant to the needs of women who have experienced sexual abuse. She uncovers how pastoral agencies, including the churches, may collude in many of the myths surrounding violence against women. An adequate pastoral response must address the structures of the nuclear family and the legal system which trap women in damaging relationships.

Drawing upon the perspectives of history, literature, and drama, Sandra Freeman explores changing attitudes to lesbian sexuality, and the power inherent in recovering such stories. She offers various examples of the ways in which friendships between women have shifted the horizons of social acceptability about sexuality, autonomy, and self-determination.

One of the recurring themes of this collection is the extent to which caring within the home and labour market is constructed as a gendered activity. Women's caring role largely receives little recognition and reward. Elizabeth Nash traces the multiple effects of gender, class, and race discrimination on the status of black health care workers, arguing that the caring function of black women is further relegated to that of servicing in low-status, low-income occupations.

Jill Robson draws on her experience of making the transition from home to the labour market via higher education. She offers some models of care and support which may be appropriate to facilitate women's self-confidence in this context.

In various ways, all five essays criticize patterns of individual pastoral care which fail to take account of the economic, cultural, and social pressures upon women, and serve to deny them adequate choices and opportunities. These factors may also obscure the strong ties between women in developing their own networks of care, support, and encouragement.

# 6 'Take My Intellect, and Use'

ALISON PEACOCK

I write under the influence of a black book. It contains the official record of my own career in secondary school. Twice a year, every year, neat columns of figures inform me of marks received in every subject, my class position and average, and the total number of pupils examined. So, from the ages of twelve to sixteen, I am provided with information that enables me to measure my performance both in relation to that of other pupils, and in relation to an external standard. I monitor progress like the rise and fall of shares on the stock-market, seeking from this meticulous system of accounting some guarantee of personal worth.

The need for assurance is with me still. I began my education as a conformist, but reasonably confident child. Soon, I became an over-anxious student, living in constant fear of failure or exposure as a fraud. I have since been a postgraduate 'non-completer', an experience which led me to reject educational institutions in favour of alternative learning methods. More recently, I have been one of the many women returners to higher education in the 1990s. So my thoughts on women and education grow from experience, which involves limitation as well as strength. I cannot speak for black or working-class women, or any other group that is alienated by British education at every level. I speak as one of the many women who enjoy privilege within the system, and yet emerge with decreased, rather than increased, confidence in their minds. Formal education disadvantages women as a group, leaving even very able individuals with a deep sense of insecurity about their intellectual capacity and value. The source of women's insecurity is the main subject of this article, but I also aim to evaluate ways in which some have responded.

Women's disadvantage stems from the fact that the British education system is male-dominated. Despite equal opportunities legislation in the 1970s and 1980s, and increasing awareness of gender issues in the classroom, this bias is still marked. Figures from the Department of Education and Science (1988–89) show that of the thousands of women and men teaching and lecturing full-time in the academic year, the only sector in which women predominate is the one which most closely approximates to their role in the household. Caring for small children is perceived to be women's work. This means that primary school teachers are afforded low status in the educational hierarchy, despite the obvious value of their work. Yet, even in primary education women are less likely than men to hold positions of influence: the more prestigious the job, the lower the proportion of women employed. However, there is no need to quote statistics to pupils. The transfer to secondary school often involves, even today, the novel experience of male teachers. The feminine environment of primary education is left behind. Thus, promotion – for girls and boys alike – is associated with access to a world in which men exercise control.

The numerical bias towards males both reflects and reinforces a more fundamental obstacle facing girls. This is the deep-seated belief that boys are more able, and of greater value and interest than female pupils. Teachers have been observed to devote nearly two-thirds of their attention to boys, even when making a deliberate effort to give girls half. Often, regardless of whether or not boys form a majority in the class, lessons are designed in accordance with their interests and needs. In *The Guardian* (1992) 'Doonesbury' cartoonist Garry Trudeau recently satirized such practices by depicting a small girl's first day in nursery school. The child sits on the floor with her hand in the air, while the teacher directs questions over her head to the boys in the row behind. The girl's response – 'Maybe I need to lose some weight' – is a sad but accurate comment on the way in which girls interpret their 'invisibility' as proof of inferior worth. This assessment may be reinforced by well-meaning, but nevertheless damaging, remarks by their teachers. On more than one occasion I was told that girls could not expect to keep up with boys after the first few years of secondary school. No one suggested that the cause might be structural, and so I believed the deficiency to be natural. Underachievement was just another consequence of puberty, as unavoidable as breasts or periods. Viewed this way, even the opportunity to grasp the nature of sexism was removed.

Benign neglect of female pupils continues throughout school, and is arguably more pronounced in higher education. The cumulative effect convinces women that they are less able than men, and that their opinions are of secondary worth. So they learn to refrain from expressing their views, and their silence may be compounded by the conventions of academic work. Paula, a qualified nurse with years of teaching experience, rewrites an entire essay because a male colleague has told her that the word 'I' has no place in a university. So her lively style is strangled, and her carefully considered arguments distanced and neutralized. Men, too, may feel obliged to obey the perceived rules of academic writing, but their confidence in expressing personal opinions is less likely to be damaged. Women, who have received far less encouragement to speak out, can do without the disabling pressure of conventions that require them to disown their ideas. I once took pride in my ability to argue a case through respectful reference to scholars in the field. Yet, in so doing, I learned how to deny and disguise. The ability to summarize and assess different arguments is a valuable skill. It is important, however, for women to keep faith with their own experience and judgement. They do not need to be instructed to show 'more humility', a comment which one woman received on a piece of her work. Instead, women require encouragement to make themselves visible, and to speak with confidence their own words.

The secondary status of women in education is enforced by pressure from outside the system as well as invisibility within. From puberty onwards, girls' futures are limited by perceptions of their future roles as wives, mothers, members of the caring professions, and workers in service jobs. One researcher (Spear, 1985), conducting an investigation into science teachers' attitudes, found that twenty-nine per cent thought that a woman's place is in the home; forty-two per cent agreed that a woman's career is not as important as a man's; and seventy-one per cent believed that women should only have children if they are prepared to give up their job. Clearly, for some teachers, developing girls' abilities is considered to be less important than preparing them for a circumscribed womanhood.

This belief may be much stronger in the home, and expressed in the greater amount of domestic responsibilities allocated to girls. I have a clear memory of a class discussion on this topic, which took place in the lazy days just after 'O' levels. The majority of girls shared in the day-to-day running of the home, and at least one was expected to make her brothers' beds before school. By contrast, boys' duties were light, and more likely to earn a financial reward. Thus girls are deprived of time for themselves, and taught to accept unequal opportunity as natural. To argue otherwise is to challenge expectations of the female role, and so jeopardize a fragile claim to womanhood.

Mature women, with the insecurities of adolescence a thing of the past, often find themselves in the same dilemma. There has been a steady increase in the number of women registering for part-time, rather than full-time, study at both undergraduate and postgraduate levels. Women are acutely aware that time given to study is usually taken from family life. To develop as a learner is to shrink as a carer, and this creates a near impossible choice for wives and mothers. Yet the root of the problem lies deeper than a family's demands. I have noticed that many single women feel under pressure to conform to the same caring model. The woman who enjoys a relative degree of freedom from domestic responsibilities, and in theory more time to pursue her own interests, may feel a strong compulsion to use this time in the service of friends. She is an ever-listening ear, continually available to others, even at cost to her own work. Indeed, her selflessness can be a way of communicating, especially to other women, that she poses no threat to conventional views of womanhood. My own postgraduate career was characterized by hours of free babysitting for wives of students in the college where I lived. The service was willingly offered. Yet, in retrospect, I suspect that my offer sprang not so much from generosity as from a desire to be accepted. I had, like many other women, absorbed the message that living for others is more important than choosing and pursuing one's own work.

Thus education leaves women caught in a double bind. They are invisible within the system, but the price of visibility is loss of womanhood. Not surprisingly, many girls remove themselves at an early age, especially from subjects like physics, which are strongly male-identified. Their absence becomes increasingly obvious: women received forty-five per cent of all first degrees, but only thirty-eight per cent of higher degrees in 1988. Clearly, the statistics of female non-participation do not reflect free choice, but the combination of systematic discrimination and conditioning I have described.

However, for the purpose of this article, I want to focus on women who make a conscious decision to reject the system altogether. They are often newly aware of the impact sexism has had on their lives, and are trying to come to terms with the numerous and subtle ways in which they have been cheated. Their experience of discrimination enables them to see the limited assumptions and flawed values on which the system is based. It leads some women to form learning groups that are based on different values, in which female experience is acknowledged rather than belittled. Yet, such groups do not necessarily encourage confidence in women's minds. Just as much as formal education, some woman-friendly programmes are likely to restrict rather than realize female potential.

Before considering feminist alternatives, I want to respond to the argument that women ought to make a complete break. For some women, leaving the system is an act of protest, intended to challenge traditional academic priorities and goals. It may proclaim that caring for other people does matter, and that the price of academic success is too high. It may affirm a deep conviction that the quality of a person's mind ought not to be the sole determinant of worth, and that systems which promote such a partial view of human life are deeply flawed. Yet, however valid the criticisms implied in the action, the effectiveness of opting out as a strategy for women needs to be questioned. It

75

cannot be seen as a radical challenge to the education system if, at the same time, opting out confirms prejudices about women's abilities and commitment to their work. It may even contribute towards the creation of a parallel set of feminist prejudices, in which a decision to remain within the system is seen as a selfish betrayal of sisterhood rather than womanhood! Most important of all, leaving moves women into the margins, so that mainstream education remains unchallenged and unchanged. Given that disadvantage still restricts girls in compulsory schooling, a mass exodus of able and principled women is scarcely beneficial.

Next, in reaction to the competitive ethos of formal education, women may attempt to develop ways of learning that are other-directed. Here, seminars are replaced by small, informal groups, and confrontational debate by discussions in which the support of participants is promoted. Certainly, many women find this approach helpful. How we learn is just as important as what we learn, and women's education programmes have demonstrated the success of both insight and method. Nevertheless, there are dangers involved. Women can easily remain in their traditional role as carers for others' needs. Hesitancy in expressing personal opinions, especially those which might provoke conflict, has been observed to be a feature of women's behaviour in a mixed tutorial. Yet, in single-sex classes, the pattern is not necessarily altered. Women's groups may reveal a tendency for participants to avoid discussion, as they attempt to cover up differences with gestures of support and caring towards each other. This situation will be familiar to anyone who has tried to raise a potentially divisive issue in her women's group, and found herself unable to do so because another member felt threatened. Support is essential to the learning process, but less useful when viewed as an end. In the long run, harmony as a prime objective means that issues and analysis are dropped.

The most damaging consequence of the nurturing syndrome in women's groups is that the intellect is too easily demonized. Feminist anti-intellectualism is very apparent in attitudes to women in academic work. To pose a question close to home, just how welcome is the professional theo-

logian in the average Christian feminist group? Simul-
taneously viewed as pioneer and collaborator, she quickly
becomes a focus for women's ambivalent feelings towards
thought and thinkers. Their suspicion is often justified, and
is in fact necessary for survival. The mainstream of Western
thought has been controlled by men, and is responsible for
many negative attitudes towards women that affect their
education in the 1990s. Yet, although women need to
question the limitations and assumptions of male logic,
they cannot afford to reject all thought as irremediably
patriarchal. To do so is to play into gender stereotypes that
keep them trapped. However, neither should women suddenly engage in the twentieth-century equivalent of debating
how many angels can dance on a pinhead. The task is to
enable women's thinking participation in the world.

So what resources from women's education might achieve
this end? Key principles as well as specific strategies need to
be considered, not just by providers of learning programmes
for women, but by women themselves. The first principle is
obvious, but nevertheless is often overlooked. We need to
begin by affirming – and committing ourselves to continually reaffirming – belief in the potential of women's
minds. This means refusing to accept second-class status,
and questioning policies and practices that treat women as
less than equal. For example, Church employees might wish
to compare expenditure on training for a predominantly
male clergy with similar investment in opportunities for
female lay workers! Moreover, education and training
opportunities for women should ensure that their opportunities are genuinely expanded. Jane Thompson (1983), an
adult educationalist who has developed some pioneering
educational programmes for women, has observed that the
philosophy of 'starting where the student is' very often
leaves women trapped. Her experience of running courses
for women with minimal or no qualifications indicates that
we should never underestimate the capacity of women to
wrestle with complex ideas. Women are creative and critical
thinkers, and require equal access to opportunities that
enable their potential to be developed.

To argue the case for paying serious attention to the

development of women's minds is not to endorse the competitive individualism promoted by school and higher education. The critical difference, and a key theme of women's studies, is that learning and other elements of life should be more closely integrated. Knowledge is not, as examination-based education teaches us, a prize to be won and jealously guarded. So learning can never be an isolated activity, confined to a self-referential world of experts and books. It must continually connect with, and be tested by, the mundane realities of the wider world. On a practical level, this will involve greater appreciation by educators of the need to maintain a healthy balance between the demands of study, family, and job. In fact, some feminists have argued that a more flexible system, which takes into account the fragmented lifecycles of women, offers a positive model for the development of education in the 1990s. My own view is that this system would be especially beneficial for men, who for too long have been allowed to use intellectuality to escape from, rather than engage with, the messiness of human life. It will only benefit women if, in the words of Adrienne Rich (1980), we also begin to 'insist that work be as meaningful as love and friendship in our lives'. This does not mean abandoning our responsibilities towards others, but claiming space in which we have an equal responsibility to be singleminded.

Education not only teaches us the type of knowledge we ought to value, but the extent to which our own is undervalued. So perhaps the most important implication of the feminist emphasis on greater integration between learning and life, is redefining what can be studied. This means paying special attention to those aspects of life that are dismissed or excluded from the academic world. For women, whose life experiences are consistently undermined by formal education, redefinition is not just valuable but vital. It frees us to own and create, rather than simply receive and 'master', knowledge. Separate provision is an effective tool but is best seen as a means rather than an end. Given the extent of male bias in the curriculum, some access to separate provision is likely to be a near permanent need. However, the aim is not to construct an annex to male knowledge, but to create a base from which women's knowledge can be validated, debated and disseminated. It is not enough to argue the case for a 'woman's perspective' in a male-dominated education system, for we need to begin to reshape knowledge itself. Then, and only then, can women's intellects be taken and used with confidence – for ourselves.

REFERENCES

Raymond, J. (1986). *A Passion for Friends: Towards a Philosophy of Female Affection*. London, Women's Press.
Rich, A. (1984). 'Claiming an education'. In *On Lies, Secrets and Silence*. London, Virago.
Spear, M.G. (1985). 'Teachers' attitudes towards girls and technology'. In J. Whyte et al., eds, *Girl-Friendly Schooling*. London, Methuen.
Thompson, J.L. (1983). *Learning Liberation: Women's Response to Men's Education*. London, Croom Helm.

# 7 *Suffering in Silence*

## HAZEL ADDY

### Statistics and stories

A United States senator was recently asked why there were no hearings on wife abuse, as there are on child abuse. The senator replied that eliminating domestic violence 'would take all the fun out of marriage'. A judge, after hearing a wife speak of her husband's violence towards her, leaned towards the husband and said, 'If I were you, I would have hit her too.' Since 1982, over one million women in the United States have sought help annually for injuries derived from physical beatings.

Unlike the United States, statistics are not collected by the British government. This was highlighted by questions to Parliament in 1989, which revealed that the government does not have a national figure of places in women's refuges, nor does it know how often police choose to record domestic violence as 'incidents' and not 'crimes'. Criminal statistics, however, show that between 1982 and 1987, of the 1476 women who were victims of homicide, 649 of them, or forty-four percent, were killed by their spouse or partner. In England it has only recently been made illegal for a man to rape his wife, but in thirty-two out of the fifty states of the United States, this is not a crime. Violence against women is as old as patriarchal society itself, but establishing the extent of it is almost impossible. It has been estimated that only three per cent of assaults on women are reported.

Behind the statistics are stories that are seldom told. Here are three, compiled from my pastoral experience. (Names and details have been changed.)

Janet's husband of twenty-five years was the pillar of his local church. Everybody thought they were an ideal couple, but for most of their marriage he was physically

80

and psychologically cruel to her. Even outside the home, he isolated her as an employee of his business. He always kept her short of money for housekeeping. The time came when Janet had had enough, and took a job as a secretary in a local firm. At home, the cruelty got worse. Janet went to talk to her minister, a woman, who said there was nothing she could do; it was up to Janet to sort things out with her husband; it was nothing to do with the Church; maybe Janet was doing something to provoke him; maybe she should see a doctor. Janet left her husband and the church, and moved to a different part of the country to set up her own business. She goes to church again, but remains angry that there was no pastoral care when she needed it.

Lucy was enjoying university life, having made the adjustment from home with relative ease. By the end of her first year she had a steady boyfriend, but soon it became clear that she was far more serious about the relationship than he was. Lucy couldn't cope with this and went to her chaplain for counselling. It emerged that although Lucy came from a church family, her father had been 'a right bastard' to her mother. He had numerous affairs, while abusing his wife both physically and emotionally. To the church people, however, he was a respected elder. 'Nobody in the church would have believed what went on in our house', said Lucy. 'My mum never said anything because nobody would have believed her.' Lucy felt she was betraying her family by talking about these things with her counsellor: she was brought up to keep things in the family.

Ann and her husband Bob rented part of the old manse. The minister had keys to all the flats. Once, when Ann and Bob were on holiday, he drilled a hole from the flat next door into their bathroom. One morning as Ann was drying herself, she saw an eye looking at her through the tiny drill hole. She knew it was the minister, who, when challenged later in the day, admitted it. Bob and the minister then held a prayer meeting, at the end of which, Bob said he forgave him. But Ann called in a woman minister whom she trusted, who said that this was a disciplinary matter and reported the incident to the relevant church superiors. On their advice, the minister paid for Ann and Bob to move to a flat in another town. A year later, Ann said she still felt as though she had been raped that day. The minister's congregation was never informed. On the basis of a psychological assessment which concluded that the minister was unlikely to repeat the behaviour, he continued to have pastoral access to women in his church and in his neighbourhood who know nothing of this matter. Bob became increasingly irritated at Ann's continued distress, and eventually told her to shut up and forget it. Ann and her friends in their outrage found themselves gagged into a corporate silence.

## Suffering in silence

Janet and Lucy's mum suffered violence against themselves in their homes for years and never said a word; Ann and her pastor still suffer in silence. Why? Feminist social research can help us to identify the processes, both internal and external to women, which prevent us from speaking out, but it will also raise questions that some Christians may find uncomfortable. These are questions about the Church as a patriarchal institution, which enforces damaging teaching about the role of women in the family, and why it is that the Church colludes in both the silence and the phenomenon. The case-studies illustrate moments of failure in the pastoral care of abused women. This chapter asks what it would mean for the Church to take seriously the pastoral needs of such women. But first, we need to understand why women like Janet and Lucy's mum suffer in silence.

One of the achievements of the second wave of the women's movement is that it has provided a critique of psychiatric, psychological, criminological, and sociological material which has attempted to explain male violence. These often focused on the pathology of either the man or the woman, suggesting that it was something in the personality which made men batter women, or which made women want to be battered! For example, Sigmund Freud

perceived women as innately masochistic, which was fundamental to his feminine psychology. He proposed that, for
women, masochism was 'the preferred state'. In other
theories, the suggestion was that a background of violence
in childhood, together with an inadequacy in adult relationships could result in adults seeking out partners with whom
they could be 'yoked together in violence'.

Feminism has discredited those theories based on ideas of
'illness' or 'character defect', showing them to be permeated
by sexism and cultural assumption, but has remained
divided and uncomfortable with the idea that some women
may 'need' violence. Nevertheless, having exposed the inadequacy of non-feminist explanations, feminism has gone
on to begin to offer alternative explanations which take
into account the effects of power structures and women's
place in a capitalist economy. Attitudes and assumptions
permeated by centuries of sexism die hard, and, though
largely discredited, these theories remain in the popular
thought and conversation, even of Christian people, as
unexamined assumptions. The case-studies give examples
of these. Janet's minister believed that Janet must be pro-
voking her husband to violence. Nobody at church would
have believed Lucy's mum because things like that are
thought not to happen in respectable middle-class homes –
an assumption found even in Church documents claiming
some knowledge of such issues. And it was an assumption
of sickness that led the Church to seek a psychological
assessment of Ann's minister.

The problem with all these assumptions is that they are
individualistic, isolated, and psychologistic. They blame the
victim, while excusing the perpetrators. Their persistence as
myths undermines attempts to place male violence within
the context of the power that men have in the structures of
society, while the extent to which the myths are internalized by women may prevent us from asking ourselves why
we go on protecting men and caring for them, even when
we are the injured party; why we collude with being told by
partners and preachers in pulpits that we must go on
caring, but that we must not expect to receive care, or
justice, or protection. The internalized oppression of these

myths has the effect of keeping women in their place. The only people who benefit from this are men; men in the family, men in society – and men in the Church.

Feminist analysis has challenged the notion of violence as simply a woman's lot, claiming that it is not a private problem that can be explained away by individual pathology; rather it is part of a much larger public context in which the power differentials between men and women are maintained in the structures and institutions of society, which include organized religion and the Church. Susan Thistlethwaite (1990) brings the theory down to earth, concluding from her wide experience of listening to the stories of battered women that, 'it was and always will be the repetitious pattern of these stories, despite their wide individual differences, that awakens me to the fact that violence against women is planned and indeed sanctioned'.

But neither Janet nor Lucy's mum have read the feminist literature. They believe the myths – provocation, sickness, 'it doesn't happen to people like me' – as do the good people at Church. This includes Janet's minister, who is unaware of her role in reinforcing secular myths and religious ideas that keep women like Janet in dangerous and abusive marital relationships. We begin to see beyond the silence of the battered woman to the silence within the family, which Lucy felt guilty about breaking in counselling; beyond the silence in the local Church – someone must have noticed Janet's injuries – to the silence of the Church structures – which erected a wall of silence around an abusive minister and did nothing to bring justice into the situation; beyond the silence of Ann's friend, the woman minister who, had she pushed the matter further, would have been accused of wrecking the man's career, to the enforced silence of Ann herself within her own home, by her own husband.

There are always judgments to be made about when and whether to speak out and when to stay silent, but, confronted by a conspiracy of silence, an individual has few choices. The silence is itself an act of violence by a patriarchal hierarchy, mainly men, against those who are seen as less powerful, mainly women. Women pay the price and men benefit. Any hierarchy can force people into silence. We have to ask whether the Church and Christianity bring any distinctive pressure to bear in this oppression of women. To answer this, we turn again to feminist critique, this time of the family.

## Feminism, faith, and the family

Feminism argues that there is in our society a dominant ideology of the family with an accompanying ideology of women's role within it. Briefly, this sees the contemporary nuclear family, with male breadwinner and female carer, as being the only desirable and legitimate family form. This form of family is held to be natural, a 'Haven in a heartless world' – the best, if not the only place to rear children and care for dependents. Since women's nature involves maternal instinct, mothers are best suited to be carers. More than this, their emotional and psychological development depends on their being able to care. This caring role is so important within the family, that without it the family would collapse.

Few Christians would dissent. There is a passive acceptance of traditional Christian teaching in which the order of Creation seems to represent the religious and matrimonial hierarchy. The authority of biblical texts such as these is rarely questioned: 'For Adam was first formed, then Eve. For the man is not of the woman; but the woman of the man.' (1 Tim. 2:13; 1 Cor. 11:8); 'Neither was the man created for the woman; but the woman for the man.' (1 Cor. 11:9). In this way, we appeal to the order of Creation to legitimize the Church and the family hierarchy. By the same principles, husband and wife stand in the same relationship as minister and parishioner, while fundamental to Christianity is the belief in the authority of one person over all others. Christians have accepted this hierarchy as God-given, and have remained unaware that even our notions of what is natural are culturally conditioned. What is natural is assumed to be God-given, which must be good. We look to Scripture and find the natural ordering of men and women there. We say that Scripture is authoritative and that the pattern we find there is normative. For if

God had wanted things ordered differently, surely *He* would have done so. Therefore, the argument runs, women have no right to dissent, either in word or in deed.

This means that whenever we find ourselves questioning the assumed naturalism of motherhood and the so-called virtues of caring, or whenever we feel inadequate because our experience of family life falls short of the assumed dominant ideal, it is very difficult for women, especially Christian women, to speak out, because what we risk is that the blame will be put on to us in a double helping. We are conforming neither to norms of natural womanhood, since we are not doing what is supposed to come naturally; nor are we conforming to the norm of the good woman, since we are not upholding Christian standards of goodness, defined as obedience, self-sacrifice, commitment, and service. Janet was told to see the violence as 'an opportunity to suffer for Jesus's sake'. Such teaching is unhelpful for women like Janet, keeping them in violent situations; what they need is encouragement to change their situation.

According to feminist critique, the Church is part of the problem, for it has adopted patriarchal principles as divinely ordained, and has taught the subordination of women. Christianity has a rogues' gallery of patriarchal heroes – Augustine, Knox, Calvin, Luther, Aquinas, Barth – all of whom advocated an unequal relationship between men and women, believing it was women's nature to be subservient. The following quote from Luther indicates that biological determinism has been with us for a long time (O'Faolain and Martines, 1974):

Men have broad shoulders and narrow hips, and accordingly they possess intelligence. Women have narrow shoulders and broad hips. Women ought to stay at home; the way they were created indicates this, for they have broad hips and a fundament to sit upon, keep house and bear and raise children.

The Church stands accused by feminism of making unequal relationships within the family seem 'natural, morally just and sacred'. The Church's view of itself as the upholder of God-given institutions, of which the family is one, is challenged, similarly the dichotomy that exists between the belief that all people are made in the image of God and the practice whereby women have never been accorded equal status with men. Contemporary psychological literature suggesting a minimal difference between men's and women's nature challenges the arguments and assumptions still persistent in the Church that God made male and female nature distinct, a distinction which traditional theology (done by men) has been peddling and exaggerating for centuries.

Janet and Lucy's mum grew up to believe in the sanctity of the family. They believe they have been allocated roles suitable to their nature; they have been taught, through umpteen sermons based on a patriarchal reading of Scripture, that they should be subservient, obedient, and self-sacrificing both to Christ and to their husbands. At their weddings – until recently, a legal transaction between fathers and husbands – they were given away by their fathers to their husbands, under the patriarchal gaze of the vicar. They have internalized patriarchal attitudes and practices. It is time for the Church to question its understanding of marriage in the light of feminism, and thus its part in consigning unknown numbers of women to a life-sentence of 'suffering for Jesus's sake'.

Feminist critique can inform and challenge the Church's response and the adequacy of the pastoral care it offers to women like Janet, Ann, and Lucy's mum. Contrary to what many people in the Church believe, 'Every three minutes a woman is beaten, every five minutes a woman is raped', and:

Far from being a problem of inner cities and working-class people, our experience of violence is one of the few things that women, despite all the differences between us of race, class and religion, have in common. All women, all day long, every day participate in the structures of violence against women that are part of this society...if a particular woman has not experienced this violence first hand, she is still subject to the litany of violence in other women's lives....To be female in this society is to have internalized a whole series of don'ts: don't go here, don't go there, don't go alone, don't hitch, don't, don't, don't. But it's still your fault when something happens. What did you do to provoke him? He's just frustrated from problems at work. It's the alcohol. The drugs. Not him, not him, not him. It's you. (Thistlethwaite, 1990)

Pastoral care is challenged by feminist critique to rid itself of the myths surrounding male violence, while women need to recognize and reject our own collusion with the structures of oppression. The role of the Bible in reinforcing institutional images, constructed by Church men, and presenting limited and proscribed role models for women, is challenged by feminist critique, which would indicate that pastoral care has a function in re-educating church people, so that women can reappropriate the Christian tradition. Janet and Ann and Lucy's mum could read about this if they knew where to find the material or had someone to point them in another direction.

## Liberating pastoral care for women

What exactly is the liberating potential of knowing that the Church colludes with men in forcing women to keep silent about the violence against them? Christian feminism is by definition reformist, arguing that even a patriarchal institution can change. If we see the Church as an institution in which the few direct the many, and in which change will either be absorbed or suppressed according to how it is judged, what hope can there be that the activity of Christian feminism can develop patterns of pastoral care appropriate to battered women? Furthermore, what would that pastoral care look like?

Above all, it would be based on needs as defined by the abused women themselves, and those who minister to them. One thing that a battered woman needs from her Christian care givers is for the myth of family bliss to be laid to rest. For most people, families are a mixed experience; violence within them is very common. Women may have as much to fear from their partners as from the stranger in the dark street. The Church must recognize and repent of its role in preserving the myth:

> It is as though we have averted our eyes from violence in the family because we do not want it to happen and believe that it should not happen. When forced to acknowledge its existence, we attempt to deny that it is widespread or severe or that it happens between 'normal' people. (Dobash and Dobash, 1979)

A church which constantly harps on about families as though they were of the corn flakes variety not only enforces silence, but also induces guilt in those of us who have failed to live up to the assumed ideal.

Battered women also need to know that at the very least their pastor's attitude and understanding has gone beyond those discredited theories towards an approach which takes seriously the power differentials between men and women. They need to hear sermons in which the violence that has been done against them is no longer named as 'an opportunity to suffer for Jesus', but rather as a sin.

Women who have worked as Christian ministers in this area of pastoral care are convinced about its potential to move from domestication to liberation. In their critiques of traditional spiritual direction, biblical interpretation and hermeneutics, sexual ethics, pastoral theology and liturgical practice, they have shown that the Christian tradition has been misused to domesticate women into patterns of guilt, self-blame and rationalization. Their re-examination, re-interpretation, and reconstruction has led to a reclaiming of those traditions such that victims are supported and abusers challenged.

Mary Pellauer (1991) suggests three guidelines for ministry. First, churches must break the silence on battering, through information and education, so that they come to realize that among their number there are likely to be victims of abuse, be that wife abuse, child abuse, or abuse by clergy. Second, ministry on sexual and domestic violence has to be seen as a ministry of social justice, which involves the recognition that abuse against women is organized and perpetuated through the structures of society, of which the

Church is but one. Third, there is a need for theological reconstruction informed by feminist critique, which asserts that the violation of our bodies is a violation of our very being. A pastoral care based on these guidelines would begin to be responsive to abused women, at the very least, holding out some hope that some of their practical, emotional, and spiritual needs might be met.

A Christian community which faces the realities of family life and repents of its woman-blaming attitudes will be in a good position to provide an environment in which battered women will be understood and supported, both practically and spiritually. Such a concern would be public, inclusive, and inviting, so that women could be empowered to come out of silence and into a community which would give them not only a renewed sense of their self-worth, but the will and the means to construct for themselves a life without violence.

REFERENCES

Dobash, R.E., and Dobash, R.P. (1980). *Violence Against Wives*. London, Open Books.

O'Faolain, J., and Martines, L., eds (1974). *Not in God's Image: Women in History*. London, Fontana/Collins.

Pellauer, M.D., Chester, B., and Boyajizn, J., eds (1991). *Sexual Assault and Abuse*. London, HarperCollins.

Thistlethwaite, S. (1990). *Sex, Race and God*. London, Geoffrey Chapman.

# 8 She Goes to Our Church

### SANDRA FREEMAN

I held Sarah's hand and felt the ancient sea and the new wheels carry us to a life we had no pattern for, that no one we knew of had ever lived, that we must invent for ourselves on a razor's edge, and I tipped back my head and sang three hallelujahs.

*(Miller, 1979)*

*This interview with a university lecturer explores how the experience of sexual minority groups is portrayed in literature.*

**Q:** Could you describe how the course you are teaching traces the cultural changes in attitudes to lesbian sexuality?

**A:** There has been a long history and tradition of romantic friendships between women, which dates right back to the Middle Ages. Lilian Faderman's *Surpassing the Love of Men*, for example, traces the lost story of women's friendship to the Middle Ages, and explores how close and intimate friendships between women have been viewed historically.

Women's friendships with each other have often been affirmed or at least tolerated in our society; but once they become explicitly sexual then, broadly speaking, they are seen to be socially unacceptable. This was the case at the end of the nineteenth century, when all sorts of taboos made people suspicious of and hostile to lesbian sexuality. For example, lesbians were sometimes portrayed as sick, sinister, and on occasions as violent characters.

One of the consequences of such taboos was that many lesbian women found themselves isolated, and often socially marginalized. So, for example, Radclyffe Hall's *The Well of Loneliness* portrays the main character as an isolated and introverted person who feels like an outsider in her community. She is a lesbian doomed to unhappiness, who in the end sacrifices the woman she loves to a man and continues to live alone. That, too, was a novel of its time; it probably reflected the experience of many lesbian woman within that late-nineteenth-century culture.

The second half of the twentieth century, when some social attitudes to sexuality have become more pluralistic, has seen a resurgence of novels which portray lesbian relationships more positively. One such example is Isobel Miller's *Patience and Sarah*, set in the same historical era as the *Well of Loneliness*. It was perhaps more reflective of an experience where two women find closeness, gentleness, and happiness together on a farm in Midwest America. Of course, there are conflicts for each of them in sustaining and establishing their partnership; but these are potentially resolvable in the context of a relationship which is more fulfilling that one which either would have with a man.

In contrast to that novel – which could arguably be described as romanticizing lesbian relationships which are best lived out in the context of a rural idyll – is Audre Lorde's about a black lesbian poet called *Zammi*. Her experience is of a postmodern culture in the late twentieth century. For her, no sexual relationship can be expected to last for ever, and she would not portray lesbian women as destined to find fulfillment with a lifelong partner, but rather in a series of relationships.

Q: Your series of examples speaks to me of the variety of ways in which social constraints and values affect lesbian relationships, and also broader attitudes to sexuality and to morality. Could you tell how those attitudes were portrayed in your recent play, *The Ladies of the Vale*?

A: Yes. This was a play based on a true story about the 'Ladies of Llangollen', two women who eloped from Ireland to a small Welsh community at the end of the last century. They were upper class, and made their home in a predominantly working-class culture; one was Protestant and the other Catholic. So within the play, issues of sexuality were also affected by class, nationality, and religion.

Although some writers would have portrayed their relationship in terms of a united, beautiful front which they presented to the world, I wanted to explore some of the difficulties and conflicts between them. In that way I hoped to highlight broader cultural questions about the links between sexuality, religion, gender, class, and race, and how these were reflected in a lesbian relationship. I portrayed Lady Eleanor – the older woman – as sometimes anxious and guilty about the relationship: for example in her reaction to the way it was adversely described in an Irish newspaper. She had been deeply affected by her Catholic upbringing, and thus was ambivalent about an intimate sexual relationship with Sarah, who was a former pupil of hers and thirteen years younger. At one point, Sarah turns to Eleanor in anger saying, 'You are ashamed of our relationship, and that is partly because you were brought up to believe in the concept of sin.'

Q: Would you be willing to describe how the experiences you have described in literature are connected to your own life?

A: Perhaps a simple illustration comes from a conversation I overheard between two men students on a train coming back from the north of England into London: 'How many women is it that you share a flat with?' asked one. 'Four. Well, no – three and a lesbian...' The other replied, adding hastily, 'But the lesbian is very nice, really.'

On that occasion, I didn't enter the conversation, since choosing where and when to talk about one's sexual orientation depends on how safe the company feels. 'Coming out' still renders gay men and lesbian women potentially vulnerable and subject to prejudice and hostility, and can often be interpreted as aggressive by those who don't share our experience. Often we are put into a different sexual category when other people talk about us, which can result in a complex series of relationships: with other women, with men, and with society.

I suppose I had always realized I was different in some ways. As an adolescent I didn't envisage marrying, partly because I couldn't imagine having an equal relationship with a man, and I didn't want to be 'owned' as somebody's wife. Although I always had close male friends, the idea of conforming to social pressure to become a 'proper woman' and marry and have children, or to be somebody's girlfriend didn't appeal to me, or seem to be true to the person I was.

I met my partner – with whom I still live – some twenty-seven years ago. As I look back, I realize how far attitudes have changed in a quarter of a century. I couldn't have predicted then that twenty-five years later I would be teaching on a postgraduate university course which explores how so-called sexual dissidents are portrayed in literature. For me, the opportunity to take part on the course was important, because my employers recognized the importance of asking a lesbian woman to teach it. In some ways, my colleagues were recognizing and valuing my sexuality, and providing an opportunity for me to integrate my lesbianism more effectively with my professional work.

At the same time, I recognize that such an opportunity is very rare indeed. Many people still suffer discrimination if they are not heterosexual, and current legislation in Britain does not protect lesbian women and gay men from harassment. It is often assumed that if we are honest about ourselves and our lifestyle we are perverting others and promoting our sexuality, rather than affirming our identity, and finding experiences in common with others in a minority group.

Q: It's interesting that what you've so far said about attitudes to relationships are often reflected in debates which I hear within some churches. Often lesbians and gay men are either ignored or spoken about by members of the institution, and sometimes stereotyped as a pastoral problem. More recently, it has become less easy to ignore the reality of gay and lesbian experience, because some are willing to risk talking more openly about themselves. Given that you are also a confirmed member of the Anglican Church, I'd be interested to hear how you experience the attitudes of other Christians to your sexuality.

A: Although I've gone through periods of doubt, I currently attend my local church on the whole fairly anonymously to receive Communion. To be honest, I feel that quite a lot of its organization and activities are geared towards people who are members of a nuclear family. I haven't made much of an effort to include myself in that community, but it is in some ways quite a contrast to my working environment, where attitudes are more open and liberal.

In terms of pastoral care, I suspect that I wouldn't look to a clergyman who hardly knew me for advice about my sexuality; but I feel that many lesbian women and gay men are supported and uplifted by knowing there are gay and lesbian ministers and priests within the churches. It's important to us that ministry reflects the diversity of human sexuality, and includes people of different sexual orientations.

It's interesting to compare my experience in Britain with the way my partner and I are welcomed in a rural French Catholic community and the Abbey we attend at Christmas. In France, we sense attitudes are more open, and there seems to be a more relaxed attitude about us as a couple, in a context where there is more integration between church and community. Here, too, the sermons and the services seem to be more celebratory, and to affirm the values of love, joy, and mystery, which seem to me to be important qualities within sexuality and relationships and religion and spirituality.

Q: Would you then argue that it is those positive qualities about human relationships which should form the basis for a Christian sexual ethic?

A: I suspect if I recognize the varieties of relationships which operate in practice within our culture, it becomes very difficult to be prescriptive about one institutionalized form of ideal. Although I've lived with my partner for a very long time, and I'm very lucky to have experienced that fidelity, it's always seemed to me that marriage is such an awesome responsibility that it's questionable whether lesbian and gay relationships should imitate heterosexual marriages, which are themselves subject to enormous stresses and strains anyway.

Essentially, I would like to see much more emphasis placed in Christian thought on the goodness and positive value of loving, intimate relationships, and that our sexuality is God-given. For me as a lesbian woman, the ability to respond lovingly and joyfully to another woman physically is an expression of my creativity. Conversely, it seems to me that relationships become destructive if one party or the other fails to recognize that they are made in God's image. When people treat others as objects rather than subjects, then it seems sexuality can become destructive rather than creative.

So when I hear about the blessing of lesbian and gay relationships in churches, on the one hand part of me welcomes the idea, because I am glad when churches can respond to the reality of sexual variety and fidelity in a more inclusive way. But on the other hand, I suspect that sexual relationships go through great changes in our society, and there needs to be a more realistic recognition both liturgically and pastorally of the difficulties which all of us experience in relationships, whatever our orientation.

Q: It seems that in some ways your experience separates you from that of heterosexual women, and that although there are areas of overlap, there would also be areas of difference within the feminist movement.

A: Although I would share with feminist women a criticism of many of the patriarchal values within our society, there are ways in which our concerns differ. Given that heterosexual women are more likely to find sexual fulfillment with men, that obviously creates a different set of dynamics and priorities for them.

In some ways lesbian women and gay men often find greater support from each other than lesbian women experience from heterosexual women. That's been particularly true of the last decade where prejudices have been reawakened as a result of the AIDs crisis. Although lesbian women are the lowest risk group within our society, many have felt a new sense of solidarity with our gay brothers, because we've been subject to similar types of oppression and scapegoating about our sexual orientation.

One of the interesting aspects of this alliance is that if lesbian women and gay men have something in common, then perhaps some gay men might take feminist issues more seriously. But one group of people who may be marginalized by both groups are those who are bisexual, because some lesbians would argue that bisexual women wish to maintain both the respectability of a heterosexual relationship and the excitement of a lesbian one.

Q: Much of what you have said speaks of how groups of people, often harassed and persecuted by social attitudes, find a sense of solidarity with others who may have been similarly marginalized. This makes some interesting historical links with some of the experiences of early Christians who, albeit for very different reasons, were part of a counterculture.

A: For many lesbian women and gay men, Brighton, where I now live, has been one centre of such a counterculture, since it was a town which had a more open attitude to sexuality. I'm not quite sure why; except, of course, the Prince Regent offers some historical precedent! It is easier to live openly here as lesbian women that in some other areas of Britain.

One of the advantages of living here is that when different types of people meet, there can be a breakdown in the traditional sexual stereotypes which people have been brought up with. Heterosexual people who come into contact with gays and lesbians can no longer distance us – and we can no longer do likewise to them. So in some ways we've found that people have been less prejudiced here than elsewhere.

However, I need to hold the reality of that inclusiveness in tension with the importance of maintaining some sense of solidarity with others in a sexual minority. For example, few mainstream theatres will yet perform plays which explore lesbian relationships; and with recent legislation, many lesbian and gay theatre groups will be under threat because of the possibility of losing funding.

On one level, people who are lesbian and gay have become a subculture, and that has led us to describe ourselves in all sorts of coded language. For example, we might ask if someone is a member of the family, which is an example of reclaiming language which has often been denied to us. Perhaps, however, in the context of this book, one of the most ironic examples comes from a friend in the world of drama. She will sometimes ask me if someone is lesbian by phrasing the question, 'And does she go to our church?'

REFERENCE
Miller, I. (1979). *Patience and Sarah*. London, Women's Press.

# 9  *Servicing or Caring?*

ELIZABETH NASH

Why is it that a white woman is remembered and a black woman forgotten when they have done the same work and made the same contribution? For example, Mary Seacole was a Jamaican nurse, whose humanitarian and medical services to the British army fighting in the Crimea led to recognition from Queen Victoria. Over 100 years later, few of us have heard of this woman, whose achievements are equal to those of Florence Nightingale. Both women made a major contribution to hospitals, both served Britain, both cared for the injured and sick – yet we only give the credit to one of them. We remember Florence Nightingale as a vision of *care*; Mary Seacole, if she is remembered at all, is a nurse who worked to *service* the sick soldiers.

Servicing or caring is one of the major experiences and activities of women's lives. Whatever support is provided by the community or the state, in practice it is still the women who do almost all the caring. Black women and white women spend much of their lives caring for families, friends, neighbours and those for whom they are employed to care. Whether it is described as care or servicing depends very much on the race or class of the person doing the job, rather than the job itself. Black women and poor women service, while rich women and white women care. This is of course a generalization, but there is enough truth in it to make me, as a white middle-class woman, very uncomfortable.

The common experiences which most women share are also the things which divide us. We may all be involved one way and another in care or in family life, but the way in which the burdens are laid upon us make for great differences. Servicing and caring involve the same tasks: bodies washed, clothed and fed; homes cleaned and made comfortable; goods bought. But to care is to do those tasks with love, and to have them received with love. In the long run, the tasks are only caring when they are in some way reciprocated. This reciprocal care may be limited by severe disability, but if the care is in one direction only, then it becomes a service. Where the person being cared for is capable of servicing themselves but chooses not to, then it will be service, not care, – unless they work hard at building a relationship by paying good wages, providing good conditions, and offering other kinds of caring in return.

## Black and white women in South Africa

It is not always easy to see the contrast between caring and servicing for black women and white women in a country like Britain, where our lives are held apart by the society and different communities in which we live. In South Africa, the contrast is sharper. There, where black women are the servants of white women, their very closeness illustrates the way they are separated from each other. Jacklyn Cock (1980) has researched the position of domestic workers under apartheid. As servants, black women care for all the daily needs of their 'madams' and their families. This usually includes all the domestic chores of a household, often from first thing in the morning to last thing at night. The white women are serviced: their homes and families are cared for by black women who also have their own families to look after. As one black woman commented, 'We leave our children early in the morning to look after other women's families, and still they don't appreciate us.'

Each woman's perception of the other shows with such clarity the racial divide between them. White women, commenting on their black servants, describe them as, 'One of the family'; 'I love her and I think she loves me'; 'She's a gem of a girl.' – The 'girl' in this case was a middle-aged woman. But the black women see it very differently: 'She thinks I am not fully grown. She treats me like a child'; 'I am like a slave in the house'; 'If she cared about me she would not pay me so little.'

The white women have very little autonomy of their own, and may also perceive themselves to be the servicers of their men: 'He gives me pocket money if he's not short'; 'One thing I do know, men should have the final say'; 'A woman needs a man to look after her and protect her'. But then they use the black women as servants to do their own servicing. They fail to see their servants as autonomous women, with families and lives of their own, they see them as children who will service all their own needs. Of course, again this is a generalization.

All the caring work which black women do under apartheid is therefore really servicing. Their opportunity to care for their own families is very limited because of the time and energy they must spend to earn enough money to enable those families to survive. As a domestic worker said, 'My child does not remember I am her mother. She doesn't love me too much and this is difficult for me.'

## Black women in Britain

Black women in Britain live and work under racism, not under apartheid. The limitations on their lives are not imposed by law, indeed the law provides them with some protection. So when they work as carers, are they caring or servicing? Is the work they do credited to them as people who care, or are they seen as the person to do the dirtiest jobs because they are servicers?

## Black women and the health service

The health care professions, particularly nursing, are areas of work where care for others is a central concern. The National Health Service (NHS) is the major provider of health care in Britain, and has always relied on the labour of black people, especially women. Without those who came to Britain between 1948 and 1971, our hospitals could not have coped with the demands made on them.

The NHS is the largest employer of black people in this country, but in nursing they are concentrated disproportionately in the lower grades. Eighty percent of Asian and Afro-Caribbean nursing staff are either nursing auxiliaries or state enrolled nurses (SEN). Many of them work nights or in less popular areas, and are less likely to be in managerial positions.

Nursing training is undergoing major changes, but since most black women are already in the lower grade areas, and few black women are now entering nursing it is unlikely that their position will improve. In Leeds, black people are six percent of the population. In 1988 they were almost ten percent of the nursing staff in the Leeds Eastern Health Authority, but fifty-six percent of them were nursing auxiliaries, and at the two nursing schools only two per cent of the 760 trainees were black (Lee-Cunin, 1989).

In one survey (Lee-Cunin, 1989) a nurse commented, 'Most West Indian nurses went on to the SEN course. It didn't matter how many qualifications you had, you went on to the SEN course. They didn't encourage you to do the SRN....Every time I applied I was told to try another hospital to do the course. They didn't even say that they would put me on a waiting list or something. Yet they told the white nurses that.'

Other experiences indicate that black nurses frequently see white colleagues promoted over their heads. Sandra, a nursing auxiliary said, 'I am really angry about the way we've been treated when it comes to promotion or pay. The white auxiliaries come and take over and step over you.' Ruth, a ward sister said, 'As I wanted to go further in the nursing profession, I applied for further training. All my applications were turned down. Yet when white colleagues were promoted before me, even a student that had trained under me got promotion and went on to further training....'

Nursing is a profession whose underlying rationale is one of care for others. However, in the way black staff are mostly concentrated in lower grades doing the hard work and without the reward of promotion, it is clear they are more likely to be servicing the NHS, servicing more senior white staff and servicing patients than they are seen to be caring for others. It is not that they themselves don't care; but that the way they are used means they are perceived to be servicers and therefore not valuable in themselves. They could be replaced anytime with anybody and the service would be the same. In this way black women's skills and expertise are systematically undervalued and all their work is counted as 'service' and given less worth, however well they exercise care.

CARE FOR BLACK WOMEN

If black women are servicers rather than carers, what happens to them when they need care? When they need physical or pastoral care, what is offered to them and how is it offered? They are users as well as workers in the NHS. An auxiliary nurse in Leeds said, 'I find white nurses extremely racist! Black patients are treated bad. One Sikh man was left wet for hours and when we black nurses came on duty at nights, they say: "Oh, he's really glad when you're on duty!" We used to change him and talk to him as if he was a human being. He used to cry sometimes' (Lewis and Patel, 1987).

Black women are one of the most invisible groups in our society. When we consider the needs of women, we mean white women. When we consider the needs of black people, we mean black men. The needs of black women, who are doubly discriminated against, are hardly considered at all.

One example of the way in which black and white women experience care differently is the question of the right to have or not to have an abortion. The women's movement has campaigned for abortion on demand without realizing that this reflects their racial and class origins. They have marginalized the different needs of black women, who may be more likely to need the right to bear their child safely. One woman said:

You only have to talk to black women – the number of us who suffer the consequences of bad birth techniques... or the number of us who get sterilized against our wishes...or the number of young black girls who are persuaded to have an abortion that they don't want and their mothers don't want them to have either....If you just looked at things and didn't check what is happening to black women everywhere else in the world, you'd probably put it down to production line techniques...or because we tend to go to the run-down hospitals...But it's not as simple as that. If they don't take any care, that neglect is deliberate. There are a lot of doctors who don't even bother to make a secret of the fact that they go along with the idea that we are sapping this country's resources, and see it as their professional duty to keep our numbers down (Bryan *et al*, 1985).

## Conclusion

We live in a society where serving others is highly regarded. But the service which men offer, to give their lives for their country, or to serve a company as a senior manager is entirely different from the service expected of women. Men serve and women service. This servicing is seen both as natural for women, and also an expression of their greatest fulfilment – their maternal instinct to care for others. In their homes, and in their workplaces, women give love and care. But their economic powerlessness gives them little option but to settle for job opportunities which reinforce the stereotype of women as servicers and carers.

Black women, with the double burden of racial as well as sexual discrimination, are unlikely to escape the position of servicer, let alone be accorded the added status of carer. They give of themselves in serving and caring for other people, but this caring is taken as service, and they receive little credit or value as people. When they need care, their particular position as black people and as women is not taken account of, so they receive inappropriate or wrong care. As workers what they do is not credited to them but taken as a right by those whom they serve.

Everyone at some stage in their lives needs to be given care. To be cared for with love improves the quality of that care beyond measure. But if that loving care is not received with respect for the person giving it, and if no care or love is given in return, then it is made servile. If it is to remain care it requires a mutuality of giving and the dignity of love. Racism and sexism take away that dignity and demand service.

REFERENCES

Bryan, B. et al. (1985). *The Heart of the Race*. London, Virago.
Cock, J. (1980). *Maids and Madams*. London, Women's Press.
Lee-Cumin, M. (1989). *Daughters of Seacol*. West Yorkshire Low Pay Unit.
Lewis, P., and Patel, R. (1987). *With One Voice*. West Yorkshire Low Pay Unit.

# 10 *From Housewife to Professional – On the Perils of Being a Woman Returner*

JILL ROBSON*

In 1977, a term after my youngest child went to school, I went to university to study psychology and philosophy as a full-time student. It was both exciting and daunting, requiring massive amounts of organization and family co-operation. Nevertheless, I got there, and after recovering from the initial culture shock, I loved it and thrived on it. At the same time, it was hard work, sometimes mind-boggling. I remember once feeling that if anyone told me one more thing I had to remember, facts would start falling out of my ears, so great was the pressure of new information inside my head.

In my year in psychology, although there were five of us who were mature students – out of sixty-five in the class – we were still something of an oddity. Since that time the picture has changed, and there are now increasing numbers of mature students undertaking higher education. Between 1979 and 1988, the numbers of mature first-year students in England and Wales increased by fifty-five per cent to 203,700. 'Mature' students are those who are twenty-one years or over as undergraduates, or twenty-five years or over as postgraduates. In fact, the statistics show that the increase in mature students is largely correlated with the increase in numbers of women returning to study. Of all mature students in 1988, forty-eight per cent of the full-timers and forty-two per cent of the part-timers were women (DES, 1991).

When I went off to university as a mature student, I felt as if I was doing something rather unusual. Since that time

* The views expressed are those of the author, and may not necessarily represent those of the Employment Department.

it has become an increasingly normal route for women who wish to use higher education as a path to re-enter or return to the labour market. Many use higher education as a transition between being at home and child-raising, and the world of paid work. They may be 'finishing off' qualifications they did not take or complete after leaving school, or they may be adding to their store of qualifications, or they may be changing tack altogether. But they probably all recognize that if they are going to get on in the world of work as returners, they need some solid qualifications with which to impress employers.

Most older women mature students enter study from a starting point which is very different from older men mature students. Mature women students are more likely to be coming to study from either a part-time job, or from being economically inactive, whereas men are three times more likely than women to go on to study from a job and return to it afterwards.

For many women mature students the entry into higher education is indeed a courageous step, because they feel themselves to be at a disadvantage in terms of self-confidence, ability to learn, and generally feel they have little to contribute. Yet as many university teachers know, the truth is often otherwise. The figures indicate that the over-thirty age group of mature students perform well in comparison with the average distribution of degree classes for undergraduates. Women in the over-thirty age group gain a larger proportion of first-class honours degrees than younger women, and in general consistently out-perform men (Brown and Webb, 1990).

In my own case, the effect of the experience of study was a huge change in self-concept, or perhaps self-evaluation. When I arrived at university, I thought of myself as a housewife and mother who might, if I worked hard, just get a degree. Such was the low state of my self-confidence. But in the course of three years I realized that I could do a lot better than that, and finished, still rather to my surprise, with a good degree. After graduation, I went on to a further three years study for a PhD. This was more for the sheer enjoyment of study rather than the need to be well-qualified for a job, although the thought had certainly crossed my mind.

The personal reverberations of such training for an established adult person can be far-reaching indeed. For me, there was a huge increase in my self-confidence. I had succeeded in academic life, an area of less-than-total success in my earlier life. I now felt the world was my oyster, and that all sorts of exciting jobs could come my way.

## Earning a salary again

This feeling was strengthened by the ease with which a job in theological education with the adult education department of a university came my way. I started work just as I finished writing up my PhD thesis. I was so immersed in the business of thesis production that I barely had time to stop and consider that the job was half-time and on a short-term contract.

My experience of finding this kind of post was again in keeping with statistics, both in terms of the nature of the contract, and the kind of work I found. More women students than men are likely to be unemployed after graduation, and more women enter non-graduate or temporary employment. Those women who do find paid work are more likely to be in short-term employment. The majority of older graduates enter the public sector of employment, including central and local government, education, health, personal and social services, church, policy, and the armed forces. Women are even more concentrated in these categories than men.

I was starting work after sixteen years away from it: ten years child-raising, and six years in higher education. Higher education enabled me to re-enter the labour market at an entirely different level from where I had left it. I had been a student nurse and a museum assistant; now I was a senior tutor. Although I was on paper qualified for the job, I was totally unprepared for many of the cultural realities of the world of work. I was only dimly aware of how male-centred norms operate within the workplace.

My own liberating experience of higher education – where for the first time in my life I had been treated with something like parity – had led me to believe that in sixteen years attitudes to women had fundamentally changed, or at least were radically changing. Also, I supposed that professional women (academics, researchers, managers, doctors, and solicitors) were treated differently – that is, as peers – by their male colleagues and by the structures. All of these formed part of my implicit assumptions which I brought to the job, in spite of the evidence that there are disproportionately few women academics. With hindsight I think that if my education had included a really clear analysis of women's position within the labour market as a whole, it would have been a much more sound preparation for coping with the still largely male-dominated world of work.

## Working women

In 1989, seventy-one per cent of women of working age were in paid employment – an increase of nearly twenty per cent over the past decade (Table 1). Over forty per cent of employed people of working age were women. Of these, three-quarters of a million said they had returned to the labour market during the previous year, having been economically inactive. In a wider European perspective, of the member states of the European Community, the United Kingdom has the second highest economic activity rate for women, the highest being Denmark (Social Trends, 1992).

These figures, showing significant numbers of women in paid employment, do not show how those women are distributed throughout the labour market. The great majority of part-time workers were women: forty-three per cent of women work part-time, compared to only four per cent of men (Employment Gazette, 1990).

At first sight, this appears to offer women more flexibility, since by not working a full working week they are having more time for their homes and families. But this hides the fact that most women are carrying the dual load of paid jobs and domestic responsibilities, and that most women who work part-time often lose out both ways. In employment they are consistently disadvantaged in terms of conditions of service, pay, promotion and training, and they are under pressure on the homefront as well.

There are also clear inequalities between the sexes in

# Table 1: Trends in the economic status of women, Great Britain, spring each year

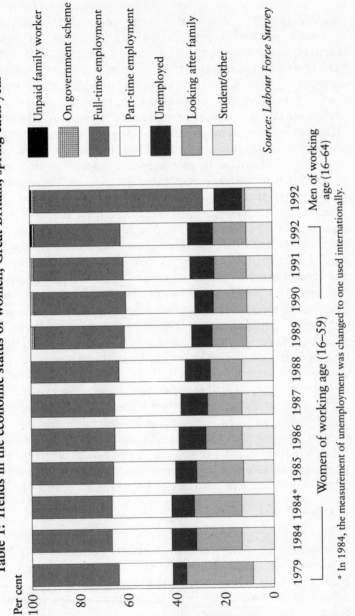

Legend:
- ■ Unpaid family worker
- ▦ On government scheme
- ▨ Full-time employment
- ☐ Part-time employment
- ■ Unemployed
- ▨ Looking after family
- ☐ Student/other

1979 1984 1984* 1985 1986 1987 1988 1989 1990 1991 1992 1992

|———————— Women of working age (16–59) ————————|  |— Men of working age (16–64) —|

*Source: Labour Force Survey*

\* In 1984, the measurement of unemployment was changed to one used internationally.

terms of gender distribution within occupations (Table 2). In 1992, nine per cent of men compared with two per cent of women worked in professional jobs: doctors, university teachers, lawyers, higher civil servants, clergy, and members of senior management. In intermediate occupations – teachers, nurses, social workers, paramedical professions, middle managers and technical assistants – the percentages are about equal: twenty-nine per cent of men and twenty-eight per cent of women; but women are concentrated in particular occupations like teaching and social work, and are more likely to be in junior posts. Women predominate in skilled non-manual occupations, such as clerical jobs where thirty-seven per cent of women and twelve per cent of men are employed. However, in skilled manual occupations, eight per cent of women and thirty-two per cent of men are so employed. Women form the majority in partly skilled occupations: fifteen per cent of women and thirteen per cent of men. In unskilled employment – cleaning, warehousing, and packing – seven per cent of women and four per cent of men do this kind of work.

So women find themselves more numerous among the less prestigious, less powerful, and less well-paid jobs. This is not because they are less qualified: if comparative proportions of women and men with the same qualifications are examined, there is still a great imbalance. For instance, in 1990, thirty-nine per cent of men with a degree or equivalent were employed in professional jobs, but only eighteen per cent of women with the same qualifications were in similar jobs. Yet forty-eight per cent of women with degrees were employed in intermediate non-manual occupations, as opposed to twenty-five per cent of men (Tables 3 and 4).

## A woman in a man's world

What, then, are some of the issues which confront women returners who come out of higher education into professional jobs? First, I want to examine some of the structural problems which confront the mature returner. Many are likely to find themselves in competition for jobs with younger male colleagues. In terms of the labour market, they may find they have suddenly moved from being under-

Table 2: People aged 16 and over in employment by Social class and sex: Great Britain 1990

| Social class | Men | | Women | | All persons in employment | |
|---|---|---|---|---|---|---|
| | Thousands | Per cent | Thousands | Per cent | Thousands | Per cent |
| Professional | 1196 | 9 | 260 | 2 | 1456 | 6 |
| Intermediate | 3981 | 29 | 3117 | 28 | 7098 | 28 |
| Skilled non-manual | 1617 | 12 | 4131 | 37 | 5747 | 23 |
| Skilled manual | 4394 | 32 | 946 | 8 | 5341 | 21 |
| Partly skilled | 1829 | 13 | 1699 | 15 | 3529 | 14 |
| Unskilled | 547 | 4 | 803 | 7 | 1350 | 5 |
| All persons in employment* | 13890 | 100 | 11174 | 100 | 25064 | 100 |

*Includes those in armed forces and those for whom the social class was not stated.

*Source: Labour Force Survey 1992*

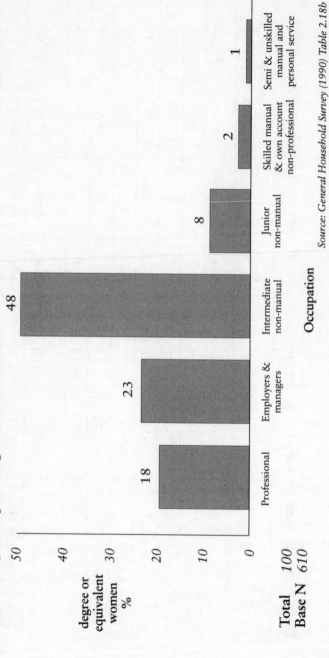

Table 3: Occupations of women with degree or equivalent, GB 1989/90
Economically active persons aged 25–69 not in full-time education

degree or equivalent women %

| | Professional | Employers & managers | Intermediate non-manual | Junior non-manual | Skilled manual & own account non-professional | Semi & unskilled manual and personal service |
| --- | --- | --- | --- | --- | --- | --- |
| | 18 | 23 | 48 | 8 | 2 | 1 |

Occupation

Total  100
Base N  610

*Source: General Household Survey (1990) Table 2.18b*

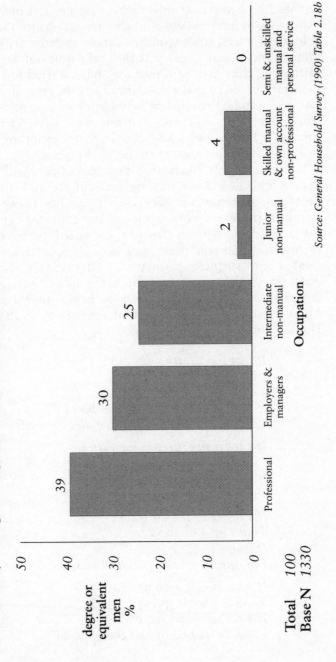

**Table 4: Occupations of men with degree or equivalent, GB 1989/90**
Economically active persons aged 25–69 not in full-time education

*Source: General Household Survey (1990) Table 2.18b*

qualified to being over-qualified – they are too old or too expensive, or have not got enough publications for their age.

In many ways, since women's career patterns are not the same as men's, particularly as they take time out for family formation, they may well find they have started too late in their profession to make much headway. In general, there is also likely to be the implicit assumption among many male colleagues that any skills women may have gained by running a family and a household are irrelevant, or, worse still, positively threatening in the workplace.

It is also highly likely that male colleagues will be the people who define the professional culture and norms of professional behaviour. There is a conflict between the norms of professional competence and expected behaviour for a woman. Women are not socialized to be sure of themselves, self-confident, and articulate, and are often treated with suspicion if they are. Alternatively, if women conform to the stereotypes of being quiet, passive, and compliant, they are often seen as being unprofessional. Many women will therefore find themselves in the 'New Double Binds' (Josefowitz, 1983):

> *If I'm too pretty*
> *I won't get hired*
> *Because I'll distract the men.*
> *If I'm too plain I won't get hired*
> *Who wants unattractive females around?*
>
> *If I wear my three-piece suit*
> *I look too mannish.*
> *If I wear a dress*
> *I'm not professional.*
>
> *If I bring in the coffee*
> *That's all I'm good for.*
> *If I don't*
> *I'm one of those women's libbers.*
>
> *If I eat lunch with my boss*
> *The secretaries gossip.*
> *If I eat with the secretaries*
> *I'm seen as just one of the girls.*

*If I don't work overtime*
*Women want special considerations.*
*If I do*
*I'm a rate-buster.*

*If I ask her to retype a letter*
*Women bosses are bitches.*
*If I don't*
*I have no standards.*

*If I agree*
*I have no opinions.*
*If I disagree*
*I'm aggressive.*

*If I smile*
*I'm seductive.*
*If I don't*
*I'm cold.*

For women returners, there is often another set of issues to face: the social or psychological, rather than directly structural, effects. For example, when I went back to work, I was in a very different position to where I had last been. While I was qualified for and could do the main part of my work, I did not have the same experience as my male colleagues in how to run the job. I had little experience of being 'serviced' by support or administrative staff, nor of colleague negotiation, nor of various sorts of networking that most professional jobs require in one form or another. But because I was older with plenty of experience at other sorts of organization, less provision was made for my induction than would probably have been the case if I had been younger and had appeared more obviously inexperienced.

In my job in adult theological education, I was the first woman in my post, and it was the first time either of my colleagues had had to work on a peer-basis with a woman: I was working in a heavily male environment, and isolated from other women as immediate colleagues. Two things kept me sane and hopeful in that situation: frequent contact with woman friends, and the women's group we formed within the university for those who found themselves similarly isolated. That group offered friendship, peer contact, and fun; and it served as a forum in which we could discuss and analyse our various situations. This enabled us to see our experience within a wider framework, and view it with the tools of feminist analysis. It made all the difference. It enabled me to distinguish the things which were structural from those which were personal and individual. This in turn helped me to devise a strategy for survival.

## Pastoring women

In terms of pastoral care, what will be of most help to the bemused and perplexed – or sometimes depressed and disorientated – woman returner, and where should she look for such care?

First, individual support is needed, followed closely by analysis, to reassure women that their problems are not just about their personal qualities and shortcomings or their inability to cope, but are structural. This makes it possible to plan a strategy for survival and act positively rather than react negatively. This requires support, education, information, space for discussion, and, perhaps above all, courage.

Also, the task of pastoral care is not just to support and analyse present structures, but to suggest something to put in their place. This is primarily a search for an understanding of those principles and practices which ensure that the work place is a good place for human beings – whether female or male – to work in. If this rather pragmatic approach is taken, then there is a real chance of change taking place. It takes a very high-minded and philanthropic employer to change work practices because a principle of justice is at stake, unless it is backed by legislation. However, employers are much more likely to change if it can be shown that such a change makes their employees happier and function more efficiently, *and* increases the quantity and quality of the work done.

It is now ten years since I became a professional woman. In that time I have made several job changes, but still earn my living as a social scientist, now employed in government. In the Civil Service, the battle for equal opportunities has gained more ground and has been going on longer than in many places – although real parity, through all levels of the service has not been reached. Nevertheless, efforts are being made and structures changed. Personally, of all the institutions in which I have worked, I find it the most comfortable place for women. I work with approximately equal numbers of women and men professional colleagues, and there are significant numbers of women in more senior posts, although very few at the top (Hansard Society, 1990).

Life at work is comfortable, rewarding, and pleasant. It is an important part, but not the whole of my life, nor my identity. There are now several more questions nagging me: 'Have I internalized the male norms of the workplace? Am I all-right-Jill at the expense of the inequality and oppression of other women? Is it worth working hard to rise higher and "succeed" in one's career, if the cost is workaholism and the sacrifice of a private life and relationships?' These questions are some of the ones which concern how we might bring justice and sensible human values to the world of work, so that women and men can participate equally and share the good things which accrue from working.

But these are questions that are raised by another stage of the lifecycle, one which the woman returner does not have to deal with immediately. They are not about re-entering the workplace, but rather about long-term habituation to it.

REFERENCES

Brown, A., and Webb, J. (1990). The Higher Education Route to the Labour Market for Mature Students. *British Journal of Education and Work*.

Central Statistical Office (1992). *Social Trends* 22. London, HMSO.

Department of Education and Science (1991). Mature Students in Higher Education, 1975–1988.

*Employment Gazette* (1990). 'Women in the Labor Market: Results from the 1989 Labor Force Survey, vol. 98, pp. 619–43. London, HMSO.

Hansard Society (1990). *Women at the Top*. London, Hansard Society.

Josefowitz, N. (1983). *Verses for Women in the Midst of Life*. London, Warner Books.

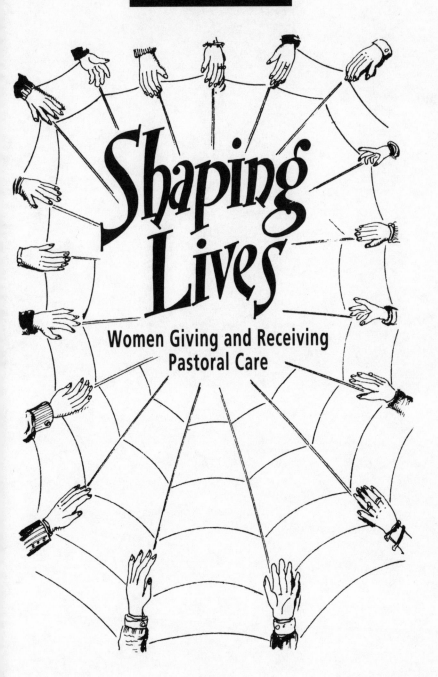

# PART THREE

# Shaping Lives

## Women Giving and Receiving Pastoral Care

This section contains four contributions which explore some of the practical dynamics of women as givers and receivers of pastoral care.

As a social worker working with families in which there have been instances of sexual abuse, Hilary Thomas explores the significance of social and economic status on women's lives. An adequate pastoral response to the financial and familial pressures experienced by women in urban priority areas is complicated by conflicting personal and professional responsibilities, and the differences of class and culture.

Liz Kirby holds together the contradictions and complexities of mothering with her reflections on Christ's birth and death and the writings of Julian of Norwich. In poetry and prose, she describes her search for spiritual integrity, and argues that practical caring involves a recognition of the pain and vulnerability that necessarily accompanies any committed caring relationship.

Barbara A. Harrison describes how women's lives in an urban priority area are shaped by wider cultural and economic forces. She explores the implications of this for parish ministry and suggests insights which 'women of the Manor' may offer to the churches.

Margaret Halsey tells the story of the complexities of working as a woman industrial chaplain in heavy industry. She discusses some aspects of the ways that class and gender affect the working lives of those in industry, and explores some of the contradictions this creates for her in understandings of ministry and spirituality.

These four contributions recognize the conflicts inherent in pursuing strategies of pastoral care which develop in response to real rather than perceived need. They argue in very different ways that caring is inevitably affected by the subtleties of the context in which it takes place, and thus call for a re-evaluation of assumptions about its theory and practice.

# 11 *Care or Control? Dilemmas of a Social Worker*

HILARY THOMAS

*Social Worker Wanted*

Applications are invited for suitably qualified social worker. Duties include conducting interviews with children (preferably while being video-taped), organizing requests for daycare for the elderly, writing court reports, chairing meetings, confronting angry parents while taking children into care, writing casework reports, establishing supportive relationships with colleagues, co-operating with management, working with young offenders, writing assessment reports. The successful candidate must have a sense of humour, perseverence, vision and boundless optimism, tempered with plenty of realism – and a plentiful supply of ballpoint pens.

*This mock advertisement may be a slight exaggeration of the range of tasks required of a typical social worker, but society's expectations of the profession are becoming increasingly complex. In this interview with a social worker based in a child-care team on an overspill estate in Greater Manchester, she explores some of the dilemmas which she faces in the course of her work.*

Q: Can you describe the main focus of your job?

A: My basic duties include being part of a generic day-duty system; working with children in need, who are either living at home or in local authority accommodation; working with juvenile offenders; appearing in court; preparing children for adoption; working with parents to improve the quality of life for their child. However, because of the nature of my current post, and the fact that the focus of child-care work tends to be one of protection, most of my concerns in this article will reflect this aspect of my work.

The child protection brief involves the investigation of alleged injuries, sexual abuse, and neglect of children. The practice in recent years has been for the majority of investigations of alleged child sexual abuse to be undertaken by a social worker and police officer acting together. This procedure is believed to be the best way of ensuring protection of the child.

Investigating alleged abuse is an extremely difficult area of work, and has to be handled very sensitively. It is crucial to keep the child's needs and safety to the forefront of one's mind, but at the same time as focusing on the child, one also has to be aware that the parents have rights, responsibilities and needs as well. The 1989 Children Act strengthens in a number of ways the position of natural parents via-à-vis social services departments, and highlights the need to preserve links between children and their families. Obviously, in most situations it is possible to work in partnership with parents, and children who are the subject of investigations are able to remain at home. However, there are certain situations where the child has to be removed from home, and legal steps taken to secure this.

It is hard to imagine the stress which is involved when this occurs. Social workers try to make an assessment of the risk to the child, consider the implications for other children in the family, absorb the pain of the child, and the anger and hurt expressed by the parents, as well as enforce their statutory duties to protect the child. The emotional context of the work is very often overlooked. I am aware, for example, that professional social workers have acquired a very negative reputation, especially within the media. Increasingly, I feel we operate in a sort of no-win context, where social workers can be castigated for acting too hastily in taking children into care in some situations – like the Cleveland Case – and then blamed in other cases for failing to protect a child by removing it from home. There is a danger that this creates a climate in which social workers may be reluctant to take action which will cause them to be criticized, and thus may prevent them from responding creatively to the needs of service users.

Q: What do you see as the central dilemma at the heart of your job?

A: Probably the tension between the competing demands of what might be termed 'care' and 'control'. Most of us came into social work with ideas about changing society, about caring for people and empowering them to take responsibility for themselves. What I think came as a surprise to many of us was that we might sometimes have to exert control over people – often people who were already feeling helpless and downtrodden – in order to provide care and protection for children.

As a example, imagine a situation in which I might receive information that a small child has arrived at nursery school with obvious bruising to the upper arm. The child isn't able to talk clearly, so cannot explain what has happened. As a social worker, I would visit and talk to the parent(s), and on this occasion find an eighteen-year-old mother with a badly bruised eye. It transpires that the mother's boyfriend came to the flat last night, rather the worse for drink, and hit her. She was not aware that the toddler had a bruise, and was not sure how this could have been caused. She states that her boyfriend, who is the baby's father, has always been good to the child, although he has beaten the mother on and off throughout their relationship.

This young mother understands that her toddler will have to be seen by a paediatrician at the local children's hospital, and that 'the authorities' are taking the situation very seriously. She has heard all about social workers whisking children away from their mothers, and is understandably scared. After the medical examination, the doctor explains to her that these bruises could not have been caused by a fall (as she had hoped), but were caused by an adult grabbing the child extremely tightly around the upper arm.

It is not yet clear who actually inflicted the bruising, but the social worker's priority would be to ensure that the child is protected while a fuller assessment can be made. I may not feel it is advisable for the child to return home that night; on the other hand, I have also observed a very close and positive relationship between the mother and her child, which I would not want to disrupt. My option in that case would be to try to find a safe place for the child where the mother could also stay. In some instances, this may involve the child being admitted to a hospital ward on a short-term basis, accompanied by the mother. Or, it could be necessary to persuade the young woman to return with the baby to her own parents' home, if I judge them able to offer the necessary protection. In such situations, the young woman may be told that if she tries to take the child away from this specified place, legal remedies may have to be sought.

This situation highlights several of the issues. My priority is the child's protection, and if the mother is not able to offer that, then other measures have to be taken in practice to remove a child against the mother's wishes. In the longer term, it may be possible to support that young mother in her situation, and there are many good examples of social work practice which do focus on the needs of mothers and which aim to build up their self-esteem. However, in the short term, I am sometimes left very unhappy about the effects of our intervention on young women like this. In prioritizing care for the child, social workers may be seen as imposing control upon the parent.

> Underlying the unease of social workers is the fact that when child abuse is suspected there may follow a radical change in the one to one relationship with the client. What was seen as a helping supportive role may now be perceived as punitive and authoritarian.... and in extreme cases the client may feel his trust in the social workers has been betrayed and may react accordingly (Blom-Cooper, 1985).

**Q:** It sounds as if there is a tension between your own professional power and your commitment to empowering your clients.

**A:** Social workers are perceived as very powerful, a perception I can well understand, even though in practice our statutory powers are very limited: we do not even have the right of entry to somebody's home, for example. Yet our job, in my opinion, should focus on empowering our clients. Often empowerment may be about offering people very practical support, for example, by making them aware of the benefits they need and to which they are entitled. The intention of the 1989 Children Act is that parents of children at risk should be seen as partners with the local authority, which can in itself be very empowering. Previously, as soon as social services became involved, parents must have felt they had lost any right to be consulted. Now, for example, it is envisaged that parents should be invited to attend case conferences, held to discuss matters of serious concern about a child's welfare. In theory this should mean that parents are able to make an effective contribution to any decisions made about their child, even in situations where the child may have been harmed in some way. However, for this to be more than mere tokenism, it is crucial that parents are adequately prepared and supported throughout the process. At the same time, the social worker must never lose sight of the needs of the child in question, who must remain the prime focus of concern.

However, I do feel that in our society we tend to push some people to the fringes, and we need to help them look positively to the future and see how that can be changed. Ideally, I would like to help people feel that they have a right to be respected, that they can make decisions for themselves, that they can challenge things that I am saying to them, and that they merit an equal place in the community.

In the context of my work, that may mean enabling women to recognize that they do not need to put up with being abused, or to accept the violence that is meted out to them. Recently, I had a client who had been consistently abused for twenty years by her partner, and I happened to remark that she didn't have to suffer this. She later told me this was the first time anyone had suggested to her she might change her situation. My comment gave her permission to consider a way out.

Intervention may not always undermine the task of empowering people who are vulnerable. I can recall many situations when, as a result of our involvement, a family has been able to change in such a way that there is more caring, more honesty, and more hope. I can think of children whose early life has been little short of hell, who have been abused and scapegoated for as long as they can remember, who have developed almost out of recognition when they have been moved to secure, loving foster and adoptive families. (As an aside, three of the most successful permanent placements in which I have been involved were with single women adopters/foster-carers, two of whom were Christians).

**Q:** To what extent are issues of care and control related to factors of class and gender?

**A:** It is interesting that when our youngest son fractured his skull and was admitted to hospital as an emergency, our explanations of his injury were accepted readily. We were, of course, questioned by the doctors, but the fact that David happened to be wearing his 'dogcollar', I was a student of social work, and we both spoke with middle-class accents meant there was little suspicion of child abuse.

I know from talking to friends in the parish and from the experience of people on my caseload that they would have been questioned far more thoroughly than we were because of their address or their accent. I am not arguing for such enquiries not to be made: it is crucial they are, but the same criteria and standards should apply for all. A recent report (Blom-Cooper, 1985) bears this out:

Child abuse is not a black problem, a brown problem,

or a white problem. Child abusers are found in the ranks of the unemployed, the blue-collar worker, the white collar worker, and the professional. They are Protestant, Catholic, Jews, Baptist, and atheist.

Likewise, survivors' accounts, and the evidence of available statistics, show that sexual abuse occurs throughout society. Why then are so many more cases detected in poorer, working-class areas than in the plusher suburbs? For example, one of the worst abuse situations I have encountered occurred in a foster home, where the family lived in a pleasant suburb, and where people probably kept themselves to themselves. Here it was possible to carry out all sorts of atrocities without being detected; but the assumption was that abuse was less likely to happen in a prosperous environment. It is often wrongly assumed that abuse of this kind is correlated with social class.

At the same time, material and economic deprivation bring problems to communities which require a greater amount of resources and attention from social and welfare services. The dilemma here is that by providing greater welfare intervention in response to need – for all the best motives – various forms of social control are inevitably imposed too. It is vital that the social work profession looks critically at the values which underpin our practices, and that social work policy is determined by clear objectives which have the support of professional practitioners and members of the public.

Q: Can you tell us more about working with those who have been abused?

A: I have had some experience in this area of work, although there is always much more to learn about the best ways of helping each individual survivor to regain their sense of self-worth and self-confidence. Although there are various statistics, it would appear that the majority of those who have been abused are girls, and the majority of abusers are men.

Such work needs to be undertaken very sensitively. The person who has been abused needs to choose how much they want to share, how fast the work should proceed, and the gender of their counsellor or therapist. It is crucial that we do not underestimate the damage which is inflicted on them, and do not make the assumption that healing should happen instantly. I believe there can be healing; but I see this as a long, slow process, with many setbacks on the way as the survivor is helped towards wholeness. However, I feel sure there will always be emotional scars, and sometimes these will be reopened.

So many young people and adults who have been sexually and physically abused believe no one can like them, let alone love them. It is crucial that Christians who commit themselves to working with the survivors of abuse recognize the need to receive adequate training and gain appropriate skills. Most survivors of abuse take a long time to work through all the grief, rage, self-disgust, pain, and so on, and there are no instant, miracle cures.

**Q:** This leads us to ask you about work with those who perpetrate sexual abuse.

**A:** I think I speak for many in social work when I say this is a difficult and contentious area. When I entered social work, most feminists felt strongly that their work had to be with those who were abused, rather than with the abusers. I sense that this thinking has changed, as recognition has grown that unless we confront the perpetrators with the consequences of their actions, there is no chance of them ever changing. If we do not at least attempt to change their behaviour, then more and more children will be at risk. However, it has to be recognized that men who sexually abuse children cannot be trusted not to repeat their actions. They are notorious for persuading themselves and others of their innocence, or of the fact that they are now changed personalities.

As a Christian and a feminist, I find this area of work raises extremely difficult questions. I do hold on to a belief in redemption and that God forgives completely, but I have certainly been in the position of telling a man that I cannot and will not accept that he should be trusted to live with children again.

I recently heard a comment from someone who worked in a specialist clinic for sexual abusers, to the effect that if somebody claims to have 'found God', then it's best to be suspicious. There is a dilemma for me here: how do I equate this apparent cynicism with a belief in repentence, redemption, and forgiveness? I want to believe there is an essential goodness in human nature, and yet at the same time it would be irresponsible and naïve to believe these men will not abuse again.

**Q:** Are there other issues you think the Church can learn from in terms of its patterns of pastoral care from your experience as a social worker?

**A:** I believe the Church should try to be more realistic about family life, and point out that everyone has their own difficulties and there is no such thing as the ideal, perfect family. It's important not to give the impression that all people are living in happy families, and that family life is one big television advert.

Also, I think the Church can be invaluable in providing a place of refuge, particularly for young teenagers. I'm aware of a situation in which one woman deacon I know offered accommodation to a teenage girl. She didn't assume that the young person in question was being manipulative or deviant, but worked with the social services to protect the child from the abusive situation she was escaping.

In terms of religious language, the image of God as Father for a child who's been sexually abused by their father is not going to be helpful. But God as Mother is often inadequate or inappropriate as an image because some abused children have been very let down by their mothers, who they feel failed to protect them. We cannot assume that motherhood as an experience or an institution is beyond criticism, given the complexities and

pressures which surround it. Yet a positive relationship
between mother and child may be crucial in restoring
that child's well-being. Various studies have suggested
that children are more likely to recover from experiences
of sexual abuse if they feel their mother believed them,
but sadly this is not the way in which all women react to
their children's allegations of abuse. There are of course
many complex reasons for this, which we cannot explore
further here.

On the other hand, it's also true that there can be a
value in believing in an ideal image of a family and a God
who is a loving parent. This may represent a real alternative to children who have been terribly hurt and let
down by their parents, and those children may be seeking
security and reassurance in their faith. Perhaps that faith
supports them through a period of acute need, and
enables them to rebuild relationships of trust with adults.

Q: How do you relate the dilemmas of your professional
life to your personal faith and to the church to which you
belong?

A: A few months ago, I went to a day at a local convent
entitled 'Rainbow People: Bringers of Hope'. As an
(almost) eternal optimist, the title attracted me. At the
end of the morning session, of Bible study, meditation,
and talking, we were all asked to think of ways we
brought hope to others. The more my fellow participants
talked, the more depressed I became! I was aware that all
too often I am the bringer of doom and gloom – not at all
a rainbow person! I sat there, visualizing the times I've
stood on a doorstep on a cold, dark winter's day, ready
to explain to a family that an allegation had been made
about the children's care; and by now any readers of the
book will have a glimpse of what trauma may follow
from that.

You asked about how I relate my professional life,
with its challenges and dilemmas, to my Church situation. I personally find this far from straightforward, and
having met other Christian social workers I don't think I

am alone in this. I suspect this would also be true for people in other 'controversial' jobs, such as police officers, those who work with people with AIDS, and trade union activists. It is hard simply to convey the stresses of a job which is, of its very nature, highly confidential. More fundamentally, I feel that churches do not take seriously the need to consider people's working situations, and the pastoral and ethical demands of 'secular' employment.

The only way in which I can make sense of Christianity most days is to hold on to the suffering of Christ. I can dimly comprehend that a Christ who wept with people, who was able to ignore bureaucracy, and could say that God's kingdom is made up of those who are like little children; a Christ who ultimately knew what it was to be betrayed by those closest to him, and who suffered isolation and agony on the cross, is the one who can bring hope to those living in misery and pain in today's society. I can somehow sense that the suffering Christ is able to be with the woman whose partner knocked her down the stairs again, after she'd given him a second chance; that he is somehow within that family where the small child is dying a slow death from cancer; that he does experience the pain of the little girl whose babysitter raped her.

I find that I keep returning to the theme of redemption – an understanding that Christ through his suffering is able to make all things new. This actually does give me the strength to keep battling on in situations which appear hopeless. There have also been times when I have known that I personally can do nothing in a particular situation, except to sit in silence with someone and pray. One of these occasions was when I had to explain to a little boy that the couple whom he believed were going to be his 'forever' family felt they could not meet his needs, and that he was going to have to move again soon. After I'd told him this and answered his questions, there was nothing to do but sit holding his hand and praying silently. There are times when that's all I feel I can offer.

**Q:** Where do you think 'care for the carers' is provided?

**A:** Within the social work profession there appears to be a considerable amount of dissatisfaction with the support offered. The formal means of obtaining this is through supervision sessions, which offer support to the individual worker as well as addressing issues about the cases on which that person is working. However, a recent study in a social work journal indicated that the majority of social workers did not feel supervision sessions were meeting their needs. It tends to be my experience that often the most effective support comes from colleagues within my own work setting.

Although I recognize that the institutional requirements and procedures have to be observed, I am concerned that all too often the supervisor does not allow the social worker to talk about their own feelings. It is a job which is emotionally demanding, and social workers often have to absorb a great deal of other people's pain and anger – and sometimes are put in situations which are frightening. Yet there is little recognition of the effect this has on people. In fact, I have known situations where if the worker shows they are distressed, this is seen as a sign of over-emotionalism, over-tiredness, and an inability to handle the stress.

It also needs to be acknowledged that working with children who have been physically or emotionally damaged, and with adults who may be violent or may have raped a young girl, affects social workers at a deeply personal level. Women in social work face particular pressures, and feelings of mistrust towards the predominantly male perpetrators of such abuse can foster negative attitudes towards men in general. All these issues need to be aired freely, so that one can work towards a more positive perspective; but in my experience such discussion only rarely takes place, and then usually within a small group.

So if one is fortunate to belong to a strong, supportive team one can receive a great deal of support from colleagues; but often they too are swamped by the pressure of work. Unless one has a loving and strong family, and/or a good, caring network of like-minded friends – and I am fortunate enough to have both – I think there can be very little support, and that concerns me. We talk in idealistic terms about empowering people, encouraging women to assert their needs and so on, and yet all too often the professional structure denies this to the social workers themselves. My fear is that unless we are well-supported we cannot deliver a sensitive, responsive service to the people who need it most.

REFERENCES
Blom-Cooper Inquiry (1985). In *A Child in Trust*. London, Kingswood Press.
Todd, I. and Ellis, L. 'Divided Loyalties', *Social Work Today*, 25 June 1992.
Todd, I. 'When there's nowhere to run', *Community Care*, 23 March 1989.

# 12 *Anchor Hold*

## LIZ KIRBY

Mother Julian and many other medieval anchoresses chose to be closed into a cell and live the life of a recluse.

### Anchor Hold

Closed in tight as a stone, here
I have a small piece of dark
where I will grow white, like
the first shoot of a seed.

A bishop answered for my coming here,
I begged him and he was pleased to say
yes. His Priest blessed me with the rites
of death; scattering earth in my face.

My friend the mason performed
the last service for me. I lay
listening to the scrape of his spade,
the slap of wet sand and lime.

Bricking me out he thought
but I had gone in.
The mortar will be my tongue.
My eyes will hatch visions.

They all turned away
thinking me sealed and safe.
They had not grasped that
they shut me in still living.

Inert, like the larvae
of a bee, I will feed
and grow huge, I will fill
out my cell to the walls.

Perhaps I have to apologize, Mother Julian, as I have borrowed your life to say something about my own. You chose an unforgiving calling; to be an anchoress, to live the

135

life of a hermit, visitors coming to your window to feed off
your holiness and leave you bread. Through all those long
years, you held to what you knew to be true: your vision.
You meditated on it, questioned and tested it, and knew
that it was good, your 'Revelation of Divine Love'. The
image of you lives with me, walled into your cell waiting
for the world to come to you. You were enclosed, cut off
and yet so powerful; growing all the time in the strength of
what you knew. I imagine that you were an uncomfortable
woman, one that the priests found hard to cope with. They
must have thought, with relief, that you would be safe,
tucked away in your anchorhold. But you never gave up
anything that mattered, and used the privacy and silence of
your room to carefully consider the right words for speaking out the whole of your mind.

I wish I had your strength, your calm clarity, Mother. My
anger threatens to turn the structures of the Church that
stand around me into a prison. I need to learn from you the
lesson of creativity; to turn enclosures to profit, to nourish
the strength that I have and focus it on what really matters.
I find the stone walls of the church so hard to live within;
they seem cold and unyielding. There is a desire in me to
work for creation, I would like to be able to express it, as a
mother, as a woman who works and is engaged with the
world, as a Christian. These are the bounds within which I
am struggling to work for good, sometimes it seems that
they threaten to crush me.

I have read that you may have been a mother yourself;
you have certainly long held the title of motherhood. The
vibrance of the calling that you accepted rings out in your
writings. If your body never opened itself to be a gateway
to life, well then your soul did. I'd like to see how you'd
respond to the soft-focus, sweet babies that are put up for
our eyes and hearts so often. Perhaps, like me, you would
feel the tears forming and want to spit at the same time. All
those pretty babies, never ill, never crying. The mothers are
the same. They always find time to do their hair, put a little
makeup on, smile sweetly when they're pegging (clean)
nappies on the line and tucking their little darlings into bed.

I curse when I'm moved by the cheap sentimental image

that we're sold. I'd like to see what those women would look like after three consecutive sleepless nights and the third change of Babygrow that day. That's vindictive of course, but perhaps you understand. My children didn't get born after a few relaxing antenatal classes and a bit of heavy breathing. They didn't feed with gurgling contentment and wake with smiles in snow-white nighties. Nor have they grown in a continuous summer where even their sheets smell of wildflower meadows and their little ailments are easily cured with spoonful of sweet syrup. I have won the right to be called mother by my children through the gruelling task of struggling to love. Like you, Mother, learning to understand how I fail and why, holding on to the thread of commitment – the decision to nurture and protect.

Christmas has just gone. I took my children to see the crib. Plaster hay doesn't smell sweet and plaster oxen don't leave steaming, pungent piles on the ground. Strange that the newborn Christ always arrives a bonny six-month child, who can already laugh, focus, sit up and lift his hand in blessing. My two loved it of course; we lit a candle and they sang 'Away in a Manger'. I sang with them, enjoying their innocence and love of a good story. We're older. We know about the filth and lonely pain of that birth, about the political consequences, the slaughtered toddlers, the exile. In Roman Catholic churches the feast of 'The Holy Family' is still celebrated with ceremonial sentimentality by celibate priests. We don't like to be bothered with it all, so we live with the half-truth, joy without pain, salt without savour.

In this way a silent, invisible censorship happens. This is why when I enter a church I want to cry, and to spit. And it matters; violence, tyranny, anger, darken the heart of our world, darken our hearts, darken our families. What is the Church if not the place where we encounter and learn to live with ourselves, naked and whole? Those of us who are mothers need to be able to bring all of ourselves to God, not just the attractive, well-groomed, cosy bits. Sunday best. What about Thursday-two-in-the-morning, when the youngest wakes for the third time, vomits (third change of bed linen), then wants to be comforted? There is an angry despair, for example, after a long day's work, when they refuse the nutritious food that has been lovingly prepared for them. Can I take that vicious anger to the golden crib and leave it with the smiling, shallow-faced Madonna?

### Nativity

They saw my heaving
belly and the doors
slammed, so he dropped
into straw and mud.
It was my own hand
that wiped the blood
from his waxy head.

An old man said I
had given birth to
a sword, but I knew,
he had already cut
his way out of me.
Afterwards he healed
me with his warm moist
mouth on my nipple,
I loved him stirring
with his first satisfaction.

He carried the edge through
long years and at last
the sharp blade drove straight
into him. At his death
I wiped blood from his
waxen head, held him
against my breast.

I can hear a number of admonitions in my ears now. For the first time in my life I am not a regular member of any congregation. I stopped going to the church that I attended when it was suggested to me that I might think of taking up a wider role when the children were safely settled in secondary school. My youngest was two and a half at the time, which meant it was thought reasonable that I should have to wait for nine years. But I am not a Madonna at all, so I left. The Church was my community, my home. But it wanted to censor me, wanted to edit down who I am. Why can I not be a mother *and* a whole person? I understand that I am incomplete, I will not be complete until I enter fully into eternal life. Until then I am a person, which means I am a mess, a heap of contradictions, somebody with a lot of flaws and an enormous amount to give. It seems that this is not a comfortable thing to accept. To blur the boundaries between motherhood, career, service to the community, responsibility in the world, is to be the cause of chaos in so many minds.

I will not cut down my truth to a remnant. It is not right to ask anyone to do so because it means mutilating what there is of God in each of us. My son and daughter are the best part of my love and life, but they are not all that I am. I would be committing a crime if I asked them to be everything to me. As a family we cannot live in the golden glow of a stage-set. Our lives are not a tableau. Until there is room for the mothers and their children to step out of the set piece and into real life, without the deforming voice of what they ought to be distorting their experience, the full richness of what it means to mother, and of what a child can give, will be lost.

Mother Julian, I remember the challenge you issued when you wrote of God 'our kindly mother', and understood that the cross was a great labour, bringing to birth a new life. How much we need to remember the true depth of what motherhood is and let it enter into our understanding! In holding on to our narrow and shallow ideas we distort and restrict the freedom not only of mothers, but also of those who have chosen *not* to have children, and of those who decide for celibacy. Children themselves become playthings, not people with their own gifts to offer. So many images and reflections of God's grace in the world are shattered.

### Famine Mother

Watching the wash day
mothers hang out their
bright sheets,then turn
to sell me love and soap

with a tender smile,
I am engulfed,
wanting to gather
my shining child to
my breast in a billow
of warm towel, but I
am swollen hard, sore,
glutted with new milk.

The news has started
an Ethiopian woman
looks straight at me.
She will not turn to
the child that licks
her dark dry nipple.

This hunger makes me
weep until I am
drenched in undrunk milk,
spilling over and
dripping into my
lap. The woman does

not look down.
The camera abandons her.
I cover my daughter's
head as I lift her
to a nipple that
has cracked and bled.

It is hard to understand why our image of motherhood does
not include anything other than the most narrow, family
context. If I want my children to grow up healthy, then it
matters that there is care available for them. More than that,
how can I be secure for my own child and not suffer for the
fate of the millions of unprotected, starving and homeless
children that haunt the conscience of our world? If my
breasts are full of milk, then the pain of watching a woman
who is dry nurse her starving child is unbearable. The only
answer to that pain is to act. To be responsible for the
nurturing of a child is to be flung hard against the structures

of the society that we live in, and to experience its inequalities, exploitations and griefs. There is a kingdom to build.

Women are so often the ones who bear witness, the ones who stand, fix their gaze on violence and refuse to look away. In this way the mothers of the 'disappeared' keep watch: without turning away. This is how it was at the Crucifixion, when the women were with Jesus to the last. It is also how the Resurrection first came to be known – because the faithful women returned to complete the work of that vigil by tending to the corpse. The women who keep faith are defying tyranny. In the face of violence they were doing what they could do; building the Kingdom. What they did was not a small thing, what they did was the beginning of everything.

### Women at an Execution

No dawn comes
only thick dark fading grey
through the sky.

Fear engrained
in the dust does not keep us
from final tenderness,

we soothe with oil
smear fragrant healing balm
on the body.

Pain hit us
in the dull blank last night
like the bang of thunder.

We stood grouped
watching violence being done,
and did not yield.

The men saw us,
as they hammered into nakedness
they glanced over.

Silent we became
an unease in the corner
of their eyes.

I have no doubt that some of the male disciples found the tales of the women after the death of Jesus disrespectful and upsetting. How could they talk like that? It wasn't seemly; it didn't become them; they were meddling in things that they did not understand. But Mary, after what she had seen in the cool light of morning in the garden, had no choice but to speak: the knowledge that she had allowed her no choice. You understand this, Mother Julian. The words that you had to say were sounding in your head for decades. You kept them safe in your heart and made sure that they were clearly spoken. Perhaps there were men who thought that your enclosure would keep you quiet, but truth echoes in the bones. Like the Gospel women, like you, like the women through the ages who have held to what is right, we must take on the responsibility of speaking out. Disapproval and injunctions to be quiet must not stop us. If we edit and distort our own reality for the sake of comfort and safety then we are muffling the voice of God who is in us.

### Advice to a Voluntary Mute

What a knot of stuttering
difficulty you struggle with

your throat twists tightly
around each breath

tongue flings its
scatter of spit.

Each word is a smarting thwack
stinging as it is swallowed

every turn of your tongue
marks how hard it is to speak

but I can hear
the shape of an echo

long vowels are forming
deep in your lungs

they are booming
in that walled hollow

will resound in
your marrow until

you sound them out like omens.

Mother Julian remember us in your prayers.
Your daughter,

Liz

NOTE
The most widely available edition of Mother Julian's writ-
ings is in the Penguin Classics series, *Revelations of Divine
Love*, Julian of Norwich, Penguin, 1966.

# 13 *Women of the Manor –*
*Ministry on an Urban*
*Priority-Area Council Estate*

BARBARA A. HARRISON

Question to a group of male clergy at a Sheffield housing estates consultation in February 1992: What is your greatest sorrow in ministry in a council estate?

Answer: Working in a matriarchal society.

When the Manor Estate Sheffield was built in the 1920s, it was hailed by its first occupants as a place of fresh air and good health, a welcome retreat from the poisonous, smoke-filled pall that rarely shifted from the industrial centre of the city. Seventy years on, over half the original houses, rendered unsafe by the use of unsuitable mortar, have been demolished. At the bottom of the hill, a mix of new dwellings cluster around red-paved courts; towards the top, the derelict ground has grassed over while awaiting redevelopment. Here and there, a lone family holds out in the only occupied house of an otherwise derelict block, waiting for the rehousing of their choice. 'The Manor' has become in popular imagination one of the least desirable areas in the whole of Sheffield.

Changes in family life have been no less dramatic. Once most men on the estate had semi-skilled or unskilled jobs in the steel or coal industries; now with the massive decline in both, the rate of male unemployment is high. Many men in their middle twenties have never had a job since leaving school. Once, the older women recall, the man of the house was not only the breadwinner, but sometimes literally the gatekeeper – his permission had to be sought before the women could go out. Nowadays, women are having to adapt to new and changing rôles, both within their family situation and outside it.

144

## Women of the manor

Manor women are as much individuals as women the world over, but for the purpose of this study, the situations of three broad categories of women will be explored.

### FAMILY WOMEN

In a sense, the Manor is in a time warp. Extended families, living within a small geographical area, may have disappeared in other areas of the country: in this part of Sheffield they are still numerous. At their heart is Nan-Nan (grandmother) or Great Nan-Nan. She has no economic power, but her influence is immense. Her home is always full of visiting family – they come over for meals, especially Sunday lunch, childminding, company, advice. She knows all the birthdays and wedding anniversaries by heart; there is always a greeting card waiting to be posted. Her family often spans four generations – women commonly become great grandmothers in their mid-fifties – and is usually large. As she grows older, the balance of care begins to tip: housebound and infirm, she never lacks someone to shop and make her meals and keep her company. But she never loses the right to speak her mind. At her funeral there will be no lack of tears, and a real sense that someone of importance has been lost.

Within the family, there will almost certainly be women who are bringing up other people's children. Babies of young teenage girls are often brought up by the grandmother or aunt: when relationships break up and the burden of caring for several small children becomes too much for the lone mother, or when a mother dies or goes into hospital or prison, the children will be taken on by other members of the family. This simply seems the natural thing to do, and there is irritation at the need to justify it to the DSS, or cope with formal adoption procedures.

For 'family' women, everything is relational. Their exact position within the extended family is complex: they are bound by many interwoven ties of affection and concern, of love and hatred. A succession of partners may mesh them in with several family networks. There is a keen sense of belonging, but often in times of crisis, the women are under intense strain as they try to care for their children, siblings, parents or grandparents. Any pastoral care which is to be effective for them must take on board the whole complicated pattern of relationships that give meaning to their lives.

MARGINALIZED WOMEN

Of course, this picture of busy, supportive/demanding family life is not universal. On the Manor, as elsewhere, there are women struggling, alone or with children, not only to make ends meet but also to make some sense of a lonely and isolated existence. Particularly poignant is the situation of girls under eighteen, who are usually ineligible for state benefit. If their own family turns them out or is unable to give them any financial help, they may find themselves classed as homeless and housed in poor accommodation with little or no furniture, and dependent on friends for meals and emotional support. On the other hand, childlessness can bring its own problems of loneliness and lack of support: women who have children who have 'got on' and 'bettered themselves' often share this sense of isolation when the family moves away to other parts of the country or the world.

This situation is common in more affluent parts of the country, but there strategies are available for coping – visits to stay with children, coffee mornings, WIs, long-distance telephone calls, voluntary work. On the Manor, women living alone are seen as not conforming to the normal pattern of family life; they often lack the money and confidence to make and keep contact with others. If they are elderly, they often feel they are the only one left of their generation.

The struggle against poverty dominates the lives of many of these women, young or old. A crisis is always around the corner – when the cooker suffers an irretrievable breakdown, or the TV licence is due, or the children need new shoes. Without the resources of the wider family to help out, there is often little choice but to take on a loan from the Social Fund or from a private loan company. It can take a superhuman effort to pay off one debt before the need arises to incur another. Not only is physical energy dissipated in the search for cheap goods and in journeys on foot to housing and benefit offices, but emotional energy is channelled into the constant struggle to survive. No wonder their horizons are narrow and there is little energy left to make connections between their own sufferings and wider political issues. The kind of pastoral care welcomed by these women is supportive, and directed to individual care and concern.

WOMEN DISCOVERING THEIR STRENGTHS

For some women on the estate, however, new and exciting roles have developed. Under pressure of the need to speak out for the rights of tenants caught up in the massive rebuilding programme, women have emerged as leaders in tenants' associations and other community groups. In some cases, training in a trade union context has provided the necessary skills; others have learned them on the job.

Alongside this political development is an educational one. Because of low attainment at school, there is a reluctance to attend formal adult education classes held in school buildings. Much more accessible, both in location and ethos, is the Manor Training and Resources Centre. This is a thriving project with a local management committee, offering courses in a wide range of skills in friendly surroundings and, more often than not, taught by Manor people. An increasing number of women are taking up these opportunities for adult learning – not only in subjects traditionally within their sphere like sewing, machine knitting and basic office skills, but also in word processing and woodwork. Despite the high local rate of male unemployment and the accessibility of the courses, there has been a low uptake by men; but provision of good child care has encouraged even women with young families to come back into education. At the time of writing, only women have enrolled for a new course designed to give access to higher education.

The discovery of unsuspected talents, and the acquisition of officially recognized skills, have brought new confidence and, in some cases, paid employment. There has also been a challenge to the woman's role in the family, especially where the woman's partner is out of work. There has been conflict and a need to adjust traditional expectations of one another. In the face of opposition from the man, the self-doubt which had originally to be overcome before educational or political opportunities could be taken, surfaces regularly. 'Yes, I know I managed to do A, but I can't see myself doing B.' To avoid conflicts at home, efforts to develop skills may be abandoned.

There is a need here for a pastoral ministry of recognition and encouragement. Imagination is called for when trying to understand the effort involved in the struggle against inhibiting factors, both external and internal, as women from the estate begin to explore their own potential. They have come a long way in a short time. Many live with partners whose self-esteem has been smashed by long periods of unemployment, or, in a growing number of cases, the experience of never having been employed at all. It turns the knife in the wound when their womenfolk acquire skills – especially where these lead to paid work. Women need support in facing up to conflict situations, and in exploring new patterns of family relationships.

The thumbnail sketches above of three ways of being woman – the family woman, the marginalized woman, the woman feeling her own power – cannot of course do justice to the great variety of individuals and their pastoral needs. They may be useful, however, in indicating that there can be no one single mode of pastoral care suitable for women living on council estates. Although they have in common the need to survive in an area of multiple deprivation and in an area that has undergone a sea-change as a result of the collapse of local industry, their strategies for survival vary considerably. Any consideration of appropriate pastoral care must bear this in mind.

## Varieties of existing pastoral care

A great deal of care, as has already been indicated, is being offered informally by other family members. Where there is no family, or no family close at hand, neighbours may fulfil a similar role, for example, elderly people are sometimes 'adopted' by families living nearby. As part of an experiment by Sheffield Family and Community Services, home helps have been retrained as support workers with a wider range of duties and responsibilities. They are local people (almost all women); and where good relationships are established with their clients are seen to be an extension of family. In the interest of efficiency and cost-effectiveness, there has recently developed a tendency to rota several different workers to the same client: this is counterproductive to trust and acceptance. Other women from the estate work in a voluntary capacity at the local advice centre and in luncheon and other clubs for the elderly. Generally, a local woman offering care, whether as paid employment or as a volunteer, is well respected. But the feelings of clients towards her can be ambiguous. On the one hand, she is known and shares the local culture – 'She's all right; she's one of us' – on the other, she is assuming the power usually associated with outsiders – 'Who does she think she is?' It was no different in Nazareth!

More formal care is offered by the professionals. A large number of social workers, probation officers, community workers, health visitors and other paid workers are active on the estate. Though often appreciated as individuals, they are disliked as a group. All live off the estate and are suspected as bearers of an alien culture.

Attempts by a dietician and health visitor to set up a wholefood co-operative have met with little success; local women have participated in healthy-cooking sessions, but have preferred chips from the local shop to the meal they have prepared. Two community workers shopped for a party at a project for women and children: they bought brown bread and only vegetarian sandwich fillings. The guests were outraged: 'I only like white bread – and I was really looking forward to a nice bit of ham.' The community workers were no less outraged at their reaction: 'We're trying to show you how much more healthy brown bread is – and to raise questions about farming methods and Third World poverty.' The party was not a success. The kind of pastoral care offered needs to be acceptable. Trying to push alien values down other people's throats – in this case, literally – and addressing questions which are not even being asked, are unlikely to be effective.

Caring – whether by family, support workers, or professionals – is therefore only likely to be useful if it is appropriate to the person in need. The level of acceptability often seems to be in inverse proportion to the amount carers receive for their services. In an area where so much caring is seen as natural and part of the gift economy, the motives of statutory carers is suspect. 'Paid worker' is frequently used as a term of abuse. Individuals have to work hard to overcome the suspicion that they only care because they are paid to: friendship and respect have to be earned.

PASTORAL CARE OFFERED BY THE CHURCH
This issue of acceptability is as important for the Church as for the secular caring agencies. Christian ministers are in an anomalous position. Tarred with the brush of paid worker and coming from an alien culture, they are nevertheless resident in the area. Though further set apart by the type of houses they live in, they are seen to participate in local activities – shopping, gardening, being burgled. As someone once said to me, 'At least you do live here.' But the pastoral care traditionally offered by the Church has often run counter to local culture and been written off as irrelevant. In a community so rich in extended family networks, activities which involve dividing people into narrow age bands do not appeal. Uniformed organizations are a thing of the past: the local youth club still flourishes because its membership ranges from babies in prams to helpers in their late teens. Family structures are such that older children are responsible for younger, and could not attend themselves if they could not bring the toddlers with them: older members may bring their own babies. This does not make for a tidy programme of youth club activities, which many would see as the mark of good provision.

Pastoral contacts are made through baptisms, marriages, and funerals, but the fleeting nature of these encounters are alien to a society in which relationships have been formed and maintained over the years. People are most comfortable with those they have known over a long period of time: the Christian minister, visiting two or three times, cannot but be seen in the same light as other professionals calling at times of birth and death. Relationships are more easily built up with women encountered on a regular basis at luncheon clubs, mother-and-toddler groups, dances, or at the local ward Labour party meeting.

The local church is finding that the more traditional forms of individual care may still be appropriate for women who lack family support. It can be valuable simply to have another adult person to take time to listen to the anxieties that weigh so heavily. The majority of a local Anglican congregation is made up of women who have no families or no close relatives in the locality: asked what they thought was good about the Church, they replied almost without exception, 'The fellowship and friendship it provides.' But emotional support and encouragement often need to be supplemented by down-to-earth practical help. In a community where family networks are so normative, there is a need to promote other networks where relationships can be formed and support given and received. Local luncheon clubs are a good way of providing interest, company, and caring for senior citizens.

There is a lot of informal sharing within families – for example, the passing on of baby equipment from one young mother to another. A fund set up by the local churches tries to provide grants or goods to those for whom the help of a family is not available. In a sense this fund acts as a kind of makeshift family in time of need. But great sensitivity is needed. Volunteers who humped a heavy wardrobe and chest of drawers to an upstairs flat in response to a request through a social worker for 'Anything at all to keep the family's clothes in' were taken aback by the firm response, 'Take them away! They are brown – and I don't like brown furniture!' Personal dignity and the right to choose can be more valuable than much needed material possessions. Sadly, it is much easier to persuade the local congregation to be involved with 'ambulance work' of this kind than in joining local protest groups for a more just system.

There are other respects in which Church attitudes, as well as the nature of Church activities, prove unacceptable. Some clergy assume that that they do a service to local people by encouraging them to get on and get out. This is often totally unrealistic. A senior Church leader, on a visit to a Manor church, advised a young never-employed woman who had completed an employment training scheme in the use of industrial sewing machines to 'Think big! You could go in for fashion designing and work as a couturier in Paris.' More practicable advice, if it involves moving out of the community, fails to grasp the deepseated loyalty that exists towards the estate. One day a woman was found crying on the pavement; asked if she needed any help, she replied, indicating the rubble of a demolished house, 'That was my home for fifty years, and look what they have done to it.' More than half the tenants who were forced to move out of their homes in the massive demolition programme chose to be rehoused elsewhere on the estate rather than in another part of the city. There is little response to an approach which tries to encourage people to better themselves so that they can move out.

Ministers serving on the Manor over the years have been committed to working alongside the community. But great tact and discernment are required here also to do this in a way acceptable to local people. Co-operation is cautiously welcomed, but there is a great fear of clerical domination: clergy are thought to be at an unfair advantage derived from their education, the resources at their disposal, and their perception by people in power. Experience has shown that they have a tendency to take over local groups. A local woman activist began a sentence with 'I'm afraid...' Teased by a minister present that she always gave the impression that she was afraid of nothing, she became deadly serious. 'There is one thing I'm afraid of,' she said. 'It's you and X [another local minister]. You pretend to be with us, but you're only biding your time till you can take us over.' It is not yet clear whether women ministers are seen as less likely to dominate, and whether in fact they are more able to resist the temptation to 'take over'.

## Women of the Manor

'As we have visited the UPAs, we have been very aware of the contribution made by women to local life, and yet the under-valuing and under-utilization by the Church of the talents and skills they have to offer.' [*Faith in the City Report (6,21)*] On the Manor there is little sign that women who are becoming aware of their own dignity and worth, and who want to work for change in their community, see the local churches as places appropriate for these endeavours.

### Ministry within a network
In the first place, Manor women challenge the notion that pastoral ministry is in the main to individuals. Women whose whole lives are defined by their position in the family network or networks need to be understood in that context. Sitting for half an hour in a woman's home may be more revealing of the competing claims upon her time and energy than a series of interviews in the vicarage study. Building up such knowledge can be time-consuming and long term: it involves a low-key, easy approach which makes home visits acceptable to the family. Ministry to those who lack family networks may involve working alongside lone women to create other networks. The congregation is beginning to twin one of its members with each person who receives Communion at home. It is hoped that a friendship will begin which will result in more frequent visits that will effectively link the housebound with the active worshippers. There is a lot of imaginative work still to be done in the encouragement of new networks, where women without an extended family can be valued and where they can make a contribution.

### A low-key listening ministry
There is a challenge too to any aggressive, up-front style of ministerial leadership. It is the constant complaint of local people that they are treated as 'all fools' by council officials and 'all rogues' by the local press. However exaggerated this perception may be, it is widely believed and deeply resented. There needs therefore to be great sensitivity in the way people are treated by the Church. In the context of local community groups, a minister needs to learn the skills

of listening, of not talking too much, and of respecting the experience and knowledge of those who have spent a lifetime in the area. It can be especially difficult, I believe, for male clergy to value the contribution of local women, since it takes a huge imaginative leap for them to value the things that women value.

## Dignity and autonomy

Manor women also demand of the Church a recognition of their own dignity and desire for autonomy. Younger women experience a degree of independence within the family of which their grandmothers would never have dreamed. They are increasingly becoming persons in their own right. They chafe at their dependency on the arrival of the giro cheque with their benefit, or the council workman to repair a long-broken window. They will not be moved by a Church that offers yet another form of dependency – on the vicar, or even on God.

## Images of God

Finally, women on council estates present a challenge as yet only dimly perceived to traditional understandings of the nature of God. These women have only recently begun to explore their own strengths and to move away from total economic and emotional dependence on their menfolk. A growing number are getting involved in the struggle against official attitudes that imply that those who live on benefit deserve less choice, less respect, and should exhibit greater deference and a greater acknowledgement of their indebtedness to the rest of society. It is not good news for them to be presented with an image of God as an old-style head of the household encouraging or even demanding dependency. The work of feminist theologians in search of appropriate images of God could be extended here. For it is not only a challenge from women in general, but from women and men together in a dependency culture. Perhaps in a community still rich in extended family relationships there is an opportunity to explore images of mutuality: a special contribution from the women of the Manor might be God as Nan-Nan.

# 14 *Crossing the Boundaries*

## MARGARET J. HALSEY

### *Boundaries of Culture*

'Afternoon, yer Grace.'
'Afternoon, comrade.'

It was the start of one of my weekly visits to a heavy industry where I work as part of my job as an industrial chaplain. 'Your grace' is not a title to which I have aspirations, but the humour which greets me when I visit is one of the bonuses of the job. Initially, for me the industrial world was a foreign land – both in terms of class and gender – one which raises many questions about how pastoral care is affected by context.

The size and scope of steelmaking is hard to convey. Massive furnaces full of molten liquid, tended in dirty, noisy, hot, and dusty working conditions; red-hot bars of metal being shaped as they move relentlessly down a production line; clattering and whining of machinery as metal is tested and ground to remove its defects. A frightening and dangerous world where women are rarely to be seen at the sharp-end of production. Secondhand accounts tell me of some feelings that 'women don't belong here' – despite the fact that during the war, many kept heavy industry running.

When I started work, I drew heavily upon the work of my predecessors, hearing much about them being 'one of the lads'. The novelty of working as a woman chaplain produced ambiguous invitations – to ride in cranes or to 'come and change electrodes'!

Nor am I sure that 'comrade' is an appropriate title for the man who greeted me. The long conversations I have had in the works have conveyed how industrial life produces a sense of community and interdependence in the face of danger. Yet the last fifteen years have seen considerable decline in trades union power, massive job losses to promote greater economic efficiency, and changing work patterns, which have taken their toll on individuals and communities.

Choices always have to be made between exploring the personal consequences of working life and its wider social implications. Often the one reflects the other, as personal and political, private and public are held in tension. A phrase sticks in my mind as one person talks of recession:

'Those in power ought to come and see what they've done here.'

*On several of my visits I am sharply challenged: 'What are you doing here? Why do chaplains bother to come?' On my more confident days, answers are easier: 'Because I'm interested in what happens, churches are concerned about what's going on at work, and I enjoy it.' 'More than we do', is one person's gruff response!*

There is an impasse in the conversation. For behind it lie a series of assumptions about differences in background and context. The 'maleness' of the secular heavy industrial culture needs to be held in tension with the fact that I, along with many church employees, represent a middle-class culture to those who work here. It is all too often that the medium seems to be the message, and that to many people, the Church as an institution represents a middle-class way of life.

The sense of alienation from the churches, articulated by those who remark, 'The wife goes, but I can't say I do', needs to be set in the context of a sociological understanding of class and culture, as well as gender. The differences in employment opportunities, conditions, and expectations between those working in 'professional employment', and those in industrial life, epitomize some of the divisions. Often I reflect on the ways that my personal history offered me choice about work and geographical mobility – strikingly different from many I meet in the work place.

For the majority of people in industry, contact with the Church is limited to its formal rites of passage at the personal crisis points of birth, marriage, and death. Industrial mission arose out of a concern to explore how understandings of God could be communicated outside a formal church setting, and thus that theology is as concerned with the mundane and ordinary as with the extraordinary and unusual. If, as Margaret Kane argues, God is to be found in the midst of life where tension is at its most acute, it is often industrial employees who experience that tension most acutely.

*As I leave the man listening to working instructions conveyed over a tannoy, I recognize the backhanded compliment, and a sharp political truth in his remark: 'Can't say many outsiders are bothered by what goes on here.'*

*I stand in another working area, vaguely surveying the computer screen. 'There's a VIP visit coming down later', one of the men comments. 'Come to think of it, could be your boss – see up there.'*

They all laugh as I read the announcement: VIP – 3 pm. Humour here can be oblique – and further exploration reveals that the 'boss' refers to God, rather than to my immediate superiors in the Church. Someone later points out to me that this offers an opportunity to get alongside people – for a woman industrial chaplain has the paradoxical advantage of not being identified with bosses, and thus being a 'guest' on male territory.

Later, the concept of God as boss returns to me – imagery stressing the qualities of being in charge, having power over others, and potentially, but not exclusively, patriarchal. It is a far cry from God as companion or worker – an image more likely to be found in the Latin American context; and nowhere near that of mother or sister – an image which emerged from feminist thought. It highlights how far environment affects the choice of metaphors people use to describe transcendence.

If God is discovered in this highly material context, yet paradoxically points to a reality beyond, it is important to break out of the limits of language and stereotype. Words and images often reflect social status, and can be subject to possession and control. Discussions I have held elsewhere about the inclusiveness of language are relevant here too, when language and dialect limit understanding and relationship.

As I reflect that much Christian symbolism arose from a first-century agricultural context, and wonder how industrial symbolism could enrich Christian faith and practice, my thoughts are halted.

*The computer announcing the VIP visit cuts out, 'So that's what yer boss is up to', comments one man laughingly. It seemed safest to leave a meaningful silence!*

*'So, where are you from – quality control?', asks one person who has not met me before. 'In a manner of speaking, you could say so', I reply.*

Working in an industrial environment raises many questions about appropriate understandings of role and function in ministry – which, like understandings of God, are both rooted in context, yet point beyond it. But unlike some forms of parochial ministry, the role and function of chaplains in highly secularized institutions needs to take account of existing networks of support which already exist within the community, regardless of any Church connection. What chaplains contribute needs to be sensitively negotiated, rather than automatically assumed or imposed.

Although the crisis points which beset industrial life – like serious industrial accidents or threatened closures of plant – are at times situations in which chaplains could usefully be involved in pastoral care, much depends on their pre-existing relationships, which have sometimes been built up over years. At the same time, such crises may be the tip of an iceberg in a highly dangerous environment. Behind any accident or death lies a series of issues about health and safety regulations, the ways these are enforced, and the tension between individual and industrial responsibilities. Often, work put into better preventative methods of care can be as valuable as meeting a crisis when it arises.

Many industrial chaplains stress, in Bonhoeffer's words, that their role in industry is to 'support man in his strength'. But the realities of contemporary industrial life speak of both human strength and weakness, and such qualities cannot be polarized as the perogative or either gender. Understanding human nature needs to take seriously how much stereotyping limits and distorts the potential of both men and women. The sharpness of this stereotyping comes home to me on several occasions – and provides one way of exploring existing networks of care – often epitomized by women's role and function within the industry.

BOUNDARIES OF GENDER
*Some time after I establish myself, conversation turns to the ways that the arrival of a new female chaplain had provoked some comment among those who worked there. As defences lower and trust develops, one man describes their reactions: 'Well, we wondered if we should take down the girlie posters. But I told them – this is a steelworks, not a nunnery!'*

It is paradoxical how the comment mirrors much feminist criticism of the ways in which women's sexuality is perceived in a Western culture, often as ambiguous and conradictory. It rings true to Ruether's descriptions of a schizophrenic view of women – most obviously stereotyped in the Judeao-Christian tradition as an objectified 'fallen Eve', or a mystified 'Virgin Mary'. Dualism of Western thought is enacted in all sorts of places!

The social contradictions in women's sexuality are paralleled in the psychological conflicts which many women themselves experience in their sexual development. In the counselling work I did previously with women, I learned how the conflicts and insecurities of sexual identity, reformed during adolescence, are reinforced by patriarchal attitudes, which encourage women both to defer to men and seek affirmation from them.

In many ways my position in the works – as visitor rather than participant – means that here I experience little sexual harassment. Yet listening to stories of women who work elsewhere, I recognized parallel feelings when confronted with situations in which we are intimidated and hold little power. Self-blame and powerlessness can be internalized;

and the task in that context is to help women rediscover a sense of self-respect.

In this context, my task is to explore how to change attitudes alongside the men I meet. As I begin to make links between women's experience of harassment, and the ways that industrial life can objectify and devalue the experience of men who work there, I find a way into a dialogue about the values which underlay distorted images of humanity. With the benefit of hindsight, I regret not being quick enough to ask what comments they imagined nuns might make to a visiting steelworker!

*There is a temporary hold-up in production. One or two of the men are cleaning up outside the cabin where they normally work. As I stop to talk, one jokingly offers me a cloth. 'Women's work this – you ought to be better at this than we are.'*

Cleaning is all too often 'women's work'. In an area where job segregation reflects much gender stereotyping, much of the paid work which women do is hidden from view, and often reflects less favourable conditions of work than that done by men. Temporary and part-time work on one level affords women the opportunity to combine flexibility of paid employment with domestic responsibilities. Yet the lower level of job security, less employment protection, and less provision for occupational pension schemes illustrate current wider trends in employment which adversely affect those in part-time work.

Further, the ways in which women combine domestic responsibilities with paid employment gives them quite a different perspective on working life. It is less easy to make a strict demarcation between work and leisure, paid and unpaid employment. Their social and psychological up-bringing – which emphasizes the importance of relationship rather than autonomy, taking care of others, rather than independence – often results in considerable neglect of their own needs in the interests of caring for others.

In responding to the ways in which people's paid employ-ment and domestic life overlap, it becomes less easy to draw a strict demarcation between the private and pastoral aspects of ministry, and the public and prophetic. Pastoral care for individuals needs to be held in tension with prophetic concern for communities and institutions. Changes in working conditions has far-reaching effects on domestic life – and vice versa.

*I decline the offer to help with the cleaning up, pointing out my lack of domestic talent, and hopefully suggesting that it crossed working demarcation lines. At the same time, changes in production methods require many employees to be more adaptable; often what is described as 'flexibility' by those who manage others could also be described as 'casualization' by those on the receiving end.*

*Walking into the works canteen, I am forcefully struck by the presence of women serving the food in the area. Like the cleaning jobs in the locality, many catering jobs operate through local contract firms – and thus caterers have been described as 'peripheral' rather than 'core' workers within the industry.*

As I sit down to eat, one of the men remarks that the food has changed quite a bit recently. 'Posher than it used to be – more healthy stuff than we're used to.' 'Healthy eating' in Britain can often only be the preoccupation of those who can afford it! Yet the relationship women and men have to food is often quite different. A woman colleague reminds me of the ways that women prepare food for their partners on the production line. Single people like myself often complain of the problems of preparing food 'just for myself', and work done on the psychology of so-called eating disorders in younger women illustrates the complexities and contradictions of the psychology of eating. For younger women, these are often experienced in terms of their independence and vulnerability, and the tensions between giving and receiving nourishment. These in turn mirror the social contradictions which beset women's sexuality. The complexities of women's psychology thus affect the outcomes of any attempt to treat the condition medically. I recall recently reading about the treatment of anorexia which illustrates how self-control and independence are closely tied up with the attitudes which many have towards food. But this perspective arises from the context of women as consumers of food, rather than women as producers. I am brought up sharp by reading the comments of a black woman writer who describes the symbolic value of food for those who migrate from one area to another, often enabling people to stay in touch with their roots and origins.

*'Snap time's one of the few breaks we get here', one of the men remarks.*

  *'What are you thinking about? You looked like you were miles away!'*

  *'I suppose I was', I reply, returning to a plate of salad and chips.*


BOUNDARIES OF SPIRITUALITY

*'I can't say I know a great deal about steel – but I wonder how on earth you function in such a male-dominated industry as a woman.' It is tempting to reply, 'It's a challenge!' and leave it there.*

As this exchange takes place on one of my visits to my work consultant, I find the opportunity to explore some of the complexities of my professional life, which are also reflected internally. Tension and ambiguity lies at the heart of most people's lives – spiritually, psychologically, socially, and politically.

  Slowly, I begin to link the external realities of my job, and the ways it mirrors aspects of changing psychology and spirituality. Just as the journey outwards into the industrial world had required considerable adjustment, so I began to discover how this resonates with an inner journey, which has been enriched by friends and colleagues. Change and conflict, ambiguity and paradox have been important recurring themes – personally and politically.

  The writer Thomas Cullinan has been quoted as describing spirituality as forged out of an experience of location and dislocation. Initially, I found that sermons I preached had drawn on the dislocated experience of the exiles – a community of people whose sense of vision and purpose had been frustrated by economic and political situations over which they had little control. Like myself and those in the locality where I work, they were often nostalgic for the past – although historically the Jewish vision reflected a social and religious integration far removed from that of a contemporary secular culture. Yet the temptation to despair or to expect a quick-and-easy deliverance from their difficulties was common to both the exiles and contemporary communities undergoing de-industrialization. Retaining a vision of hope and patience is one which is crucial to those who could be described as victims of a changing industrial culture.

Paradoxically enough, it has been through reading some of the mystics who recognized the importance of living with impasse that I have begun to live with my own conflicts – and those of the community where I work.

*One evening in a worship group I attend someone begins the evening's meditation by placing a brick on the table and surrounding it with fragments of glass. 'This was thrown through our church window last night. I thought we could explore what anger meant to us – both as those on the giving and receiving end of it.'*

Anger is perhaps the emotion with which I feel least at ease. Fear and sadness, laughter and celebration all seem to come more comfortably to me – even if not always appropriately expressed. It is hard to handle other people's anger with me, and likewise mine with other people. It has been a tough journey to grow beyond the assumption which I hold in common with many women that anger is inevitably associated with destruction and guilt, fear of loss, and broken relationships.

There are obviously many ways in which anger can be misused, denied, or misdirected – and the consequences can be a major cause of psychological disorder. Women often internalize their anger as depression, which reflects a sense of powerlessness and loss of self-worth – as an emotion it is often more stereotypically and acceptably expressed by men.

In the industrial context where I work, conflict and anger

had been part of the history – and expressed more readily and directly than many situations to which I have previously been accustomed. What for some is a sign of 'industrial militancy' – and there is remarkably little of that these days – is for others 'conflict in a just cause', of defending jobs, or of safeguarding futures. Anger and conflict thus need to be seen in the context of political power. They are not values in itself, but one which arises out of a commitment to certain values.

Barbel van Wartenberg Potter explores how anger related to her commitment to justice and peace, to use energy creatively as a force for change. For her, 'Anger lay at the heart of theology – a fire which glowed within, but something which was untaught within the theology faculty.'

*At the end of the evening, each person was invited to pick up a piece of glass and break it into a bucket at the foot of the Cross...*

*The preparation of a Holy Week service with two colleagues, makes me see afresh the importance of the women in the story of the Crucifixion. An unknown woman had annointed Jesus, a servant girl had confronted Peter, Pilate's wife had dreamed of Jesus's innocence, the daughters of Jerusalem had wept on the road to the Cross, Jesus had addressed his mother from the Cross, and women had played a major part in his burial.*

Like the places in which I work, women here were part of an apparently androcentric story, and their contributions and insights could all too easily be overlooked. The qualities of anointing, confronting, dreaming and weeping, are as humanly important as the part which the male disciples had played in the story, and were part of the process of human redemption.

In an industrial environment, many of those qualities have become dualistically stereotyped as feminine, and it is hardly likely they could literally be enacted there! Yet they need to be recognized and worked out in the world, rather than relegated to the domesticated palliatives of a privatized religion for the spiritually literate. Hidden and apparently

# Crossing the Boundaries

marginal people – with the qualities they represent and enact – often hold potential seeds of social change, just as spiritual and psychological change is often forged from experiences that people have denied or buried.

Here perhaps is a foundation for a pastoral care which rectifies the imbalance between stereotypically masculine and feminine, personally and politically. It could be argued that this task begins the work of redeeming grace, described by Mary Grey as that of: '... claiming power in relation, the power which reclaims passion and sexual energy for the making of right relations, which drives to justice, the power which stands with, protests, struggles, which bursts the bonds of unjust institutions; but which also loves remembers and grieves.'

*The greeting, 'Afternoon, yer Grace', with which this writing began, seems on reflection to hold rather an awesome level of meaning and responsibility. It is a relief to recognize that the quality of grace is often mediated through communities of sisters, brothers, and comrades.*

REFERENCES

Ernst, S. and Macquire, M. (1987). *Living with the Sphinx*. London, Women's Press.
Grey, M. (1989). *Redeeming the Dream*. London, SPCK.
Kane, M. (1983). *Gospel in Industrial Society*. London, SCM Press.
van Wartenberg Potter, B. (1987). *We will not hang our harps on the willows*. Geneva, World Council of Churches.

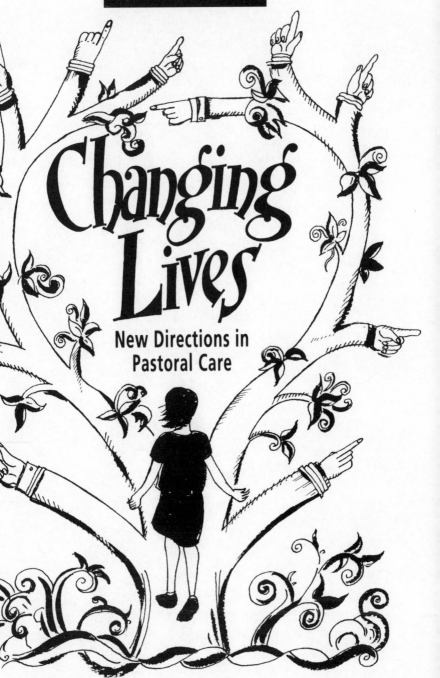

PART FOUR

# Changing Lives

## New Directions in Pastoral Care

The final section explores how women within and on the edges of the Christian tradition are seeking new models of pastoral care. All the contributions in this section are also, in different ways, studies in the possibilities for developing new pastoral theologies out of practice.

Jan Berry explores how worship is integrally connected with the practice of care. She discusses how theological models of caring may be reappropriated to facilitate women's growth towards greater maturity and wholeness.

Thelma Aldcroft develops a specific understanding of how worship speaks to the experience of giving birth. She argues that liturgy, as a vehicle of pastoral care, needs to take seriously the realities of women's lives in promoting healing and self-acceptance.

Heather Walton explores aspects of story-telling as a means of enabling women to make greater sense of their experience. She discusses the problems and contradictions which are generated when contemporary women's literature is set alongside the biblical story, yet argues that it may be possible to generate a creative synthesis which speaks authentically to women's lives.

Susan Parsons argues that training for the ordained ministry tends to be informed by gender stereotypes which reflect and reinforce women's subordination and dependency. She explores the institutional patterns which perpetuate this state of affairs, and suggests three models of the Church within which women's ministry may develop more fully. Thus pastoral ministry is directed towards building a transformed human community, whose collective life is a reflection of the essential truths of the Gospel.

Elaine Graham concludes the collection by linking the concerns of women and pastoral care with emerging themes in pastoral theology. She argues that pastoral care may be understood as the expression of the fundamental values of the Christian community, and that their enactment in human relationships is the means by which Christians disclose the purposes and actions of God in human affairs. Thus, pastoral care may be regarded as a summons to patterns of individual destiny and human community which are grounded in the ultimate reality of the Divine.

# 15  *Liberating Worship – Pastoral Liturgy and the Empowering of Women*

JAN BERRY

*Worship and pastoral care are often seen as different, if complementary, aspects of the life of the Christian community. In this essay, I examine the connection between and integration of these two facets of Christian life, particularly in relation to a feminist understanding of women's experience. I look at the models of pastoral care which are suggested by the images of God we use in worship, and why I believe that many of these are unhelpful to women in our society. Finally, I explore some of the ways in which feminist writers and groups are beginning to reclaim the tradition and construct alternative, more liberating ways of worshipping.*

### Christa

When a child is betrayed
abused by one she had loved and trusted
trapped in lies and conflicting emotions –
Is Christ betrayed again by the kiss of Judas?

When a girl is silenced
struck dumb by the terror that has assaulted her
hiding it in shame from her own consciousness –
Is Christ silent again in the courts of judgement?

When a woman is beaten
battered and ground down into fear and submission,
her face and body scarred with cuts and bruises –
Is Christ flogged again at the hands of men?

When a woman is raped
her body penetrated and violated
her sense of self-honour ripped apart –
Is Christ pierced again with nails and spear?

When a woman abandons God
crying out in anger because she is forsaken
outraged at the dereliction she has endured –
Is Christ crucified again on the cross of man's power?

And when women rise up
victims no longer, but survivors
celebrating their own strength
claiming the morning for their own –
Is Christ risen too?

This poem poses the question of whether women who have experienced rape and abuse at the hands of men can find their sufferings in the passion of Christ. It is a question with which any form of pastoral liturgy has to wrestle. If worship is to be liberating and empowering for women in a Western patriarchal society, then it must be worship which speaks at the depth of pastoral need and experience.

The nature of worship means that what happens there is vital to our understanding of God. We cannot encompass the reality that we label 'God' within language – all we can do is to use symbols, images, and metaphors drawn from what we know. Sallie McFague (1987) has argued that imagery and symbolism work at a deeper-than-rational level – they affect our feelings and emotions, our understanding of ourselves, the ways in which we perceive and relate to others. This applies to all religious language, but is particularly relevant to public worship and liturgy, where there is so much that takes us beyond the purely rational and cerebral. The language of worship is rhythmic and poetic, the words of hymns, psalms and chants are accompanied by music, we experience the visual symbolism of sacraments, pictures and the buildings themselves. The images and language with which we are confronted in public or corporate worship affect the way we think of God in both our theological reflection and our personal spirituality. It requires a tremendous shift of consciousness – often disturbing and initially threatening – to break out of the traditional mould of the church's liturgy and see God in other ways.

The depth and significance of this kind of change in our thinking can be seen in the resistance to suggestions to change the pronouns used for God to include the female, or to attempts to talk of God as mother as well as father. But the change, however difficult, has to be attempted. If there is to be an integration of spirituality and pastoral care, of our understanding of God and our relationships with others, then women need images of God, of God's love, of God's desire for justice, which speak positively of their experience in struggling for liberation and wholeness.

With this in mind, I want to look at some of the images of God offered by traditional Christianity, to see what messages they convey about women and their relationships, to see whether as a woman working for liberation I can still use them. I want too to look at some of the attempts being made to reclaim, reinterpret, and discover alternative images that can express more adequately concepts of pastoral care that are liberating and affirming for women.

One image that is problematic for many women is the one which has given its name to pastoral care – that of a shepherd looking after sheep. This is an image that has become enshrined in Christian thought, not only as an image of God, but as a model of human 'pastoral' care. Even leaving aside the recognition that pictures of a shepherd peacefully watching over his flock in a verdant pasture are sentimental and romanticized, compared to the arduous and tough existence of a Middle Eastern shepherd at the time of Jesus (or even that of a contemporary Yorkshire hill farmer) it is an image that is less than helpful. Sheep are usually characterized as silly creatures, prone to going astray, blindly following one another, and needing to be rounded up by men and dogs. Whether or not such characterizations are a fair depiction of the ways of sheep is in a sense irrelevant; these are the associations that for most of us are firmly fixed in our minds. Seeing ourselves as sheep is hardly likely to help human beings to affirm their strength of character, sensitivity, responsibility or will to act – and to characterize some as shepherds of others seems condescending, if not insulting, to those who are defined as the 'flock'. I suspect it is too late to erase the words 'pastor' and 'pastoral' from our Christian vocabulary, but as a feminist I want to challenge the underlying images, and look for ways of talking about care which are consistent with a positive and affirming attitude to women's strength.

Another concept which has shaped our understanding of Christian pastoral care is that of service. The ideal of unassuming service – unconditional, making no demands, abrogating all privilege – is frequently held up as a model of pastoral care to be emulated by individuals and by the Church as a community. In its biblical origins (particularly in the Synoptic Gospels) the image of service was radical and subversive; it challenged those who claimed positions of leadership and privilege to respect others and to practise unassuming self-giving. In a patriarchal context, however, we need to put this image alongside our contemporary use of the word 'service'. Women's service takes place in the home, or unpaid in the community, caring for children or elderly relatives. Women are frequently to be found working in service industries, where work is low paid, part time and vulnerable to fluctuation according to the season or the market.

The concept of dedicated service and vocation has often been used to justify low pay and poor conditions in professions such as nursing and teaching. Ann Borrowdale (1989) has argued convincingly that Christian concepts of service have been used to justify the exploitation of women's work, both paid and unpaid. They are reinforced by Christian teaching about submission to God, self-denial and sacrificial self-giving. This means that such service rarely has any sense of mutuality: those who serve do all the giving, subsuming their own needs and desires to those of others; and those who are served are reduced to passivity, perceived as having nothing to give and nothing to teach. Therefore, when exhortations about service are addressed to those who have no power, they act to reinforce their oppression and to give it a religious legitimization. The model of service in pastoral care is one which needs to be resisted by feminist thinking and used only in its Gospel sense of confronting claims of privilege and hierarchical power.

Next, I want to highlight those images which represent pastoral care as a form of rescuing the victim. Such images derive their power from the understanding of Christ as the Saviour who rescues from sin and suffering. It is a metaphor which even when it is not explicit underlies much of our prayer, for ourselves and for others, and so colours our understanding of what pastoral care is all about. I do not want to deny or belittle those experiences when in desperation we feel there is nothing we can do for ourselves, and long for someone to come to the rescue. But I have come to realize that for many, 'salvation' comes through the recognition of their own strength and resources. I am sure that those who help most are not those who rescue and put things right, but those who enable others to discover the strength and courage to transform their own situation. This is an insight which those who choose to call themselves survivors, rather than victims, of incest or rape have highlighted for us; it is a determinative principle in much counselling theory and pastoral practice. Women who have been victims for long enough do not need images of a God who encourages them to continue to see themselves in that light, but images of a God who can enable them to find and use the power and strength they themselves have.

Shepherds and sheep, servants and the served, victims being rescued – all are models of pastoral care which derive from a framework of hierarchical power, a context in which some are superior, stronger, more powerful than others. They speak of power-over, even if they speak of that power being used benevolently and helpfully.

Feminist thinkers have begun to develop different ways of thinking about power. Some speak of power-within to convey the power and resources women have within themselves. Although this is a helpful direction of thought, it is too individualistic to convey the concern for social justice which is so often an element in pastoral care. We need in addition an understanding of power-in-relation – that sense that we can strengthen and care for one another and our world through the power of relatedness, of partnership, of mutuality. There is a need to develop images of God's activity which can help to affirm both power-within and power-in-relation.

It is not necessary to abandon the Christian tradition in order to do this. Many Christian feminists are finding it possible to reclaim images from the tradition, to reinterpret them in ways that are authentic and creative. The historical tradition need not be one which binds and constrains, something fixed and definitive, but can be, and always has been, open to reshaping and development.

One metaphor of God's activity which can be reclaimed in this way is that of healing. (I am not thinking of healing as miraculous divine intervention, for this usage falls into the same category as the victim/rescuer images, and raises both theological and pastoral questions.) The concept of healing can speak to women who have been hurt and wounded in a patriarchal society and a patriarchal Church. Many women have been wounded; pastoral care is often about supporting women who have been hurt by what has been done to them by men. There is a need for healing which can help women to regain their self-respect and their love for their own bodies. There is, moreover, a need for healing of those wounds which have been deepened by the condemnation of the Church. Such healing is far more than a soothing or comforting process. It cannot be simply a bandaging-up of the wounds, but must make space for a recognition of the legitimacy, the God-givenness, of anger against what is done to women – sometimes in the name of God – in a patriarchal society. Through such anger women may come to discover their healing power-within, and their power in relation with other women. An image of God as healer can provide a model of pastoral care which helps women to reaffirm their integrity and wholeness.

An image of God that has often been neglected or devalued is that of God as friend. It is one that has sometimes been over-sentimentalized, and can be individualistic. It can be used, however, to convey a strong sense of power-in-relation. It implies an equality, a mutual sharing, almost a taken-for-grantedness, that is a vivid metaphor of God's relatedness to the world. Unlike the victim/rescuer images, friendship is not one-sided; there is a mutuality about it. To think of God as friend is to think of a God with whom we work and co-operate, a God to whom we give, a God who provides us with an image of care rooted in our everyday sharing. To think of God as friend provides a model for human pastoral caring which stresses strength and mutuality, rather than helplessness and dependence.

The predominance of the image of God as father in the Christian tradition has inevitably led to attempts to think of God as mother. The image of God as mother, however, provides ambivalent feelings for many women. Sometimes it is used in ways which simply confirm stereotypes of the feminine – for example, to speak of a God who is tender, nurturing, and compassionate. Furthermore, women's relationships with their own mothers are not necessarily any less problematic than those with their fathers. When women turn to their own experience of mothering, it is often one of pain, frustration, limitation, and exclusion.

These negative aspects of mothering may give us clues as to how we can use this image. It speaks of a care which is costly and involved – not a detached rescuer from on high, but someone who suffers with our hurt. That mixture of anxiety and anger which parents feel when they watch their children going against them and making mistakes may give us insights into what we mean when we talk of God's purpose for wholeness, and God's anger when that purpose is frustrated. The struggle to love and yet at the same time allow freedom can speak powerfully both of God's relation to the world and of a model of pastoral care which resists dependency and encourages freedom.

Finally, I want to suggest an image of God in solidarity with Creation. 'Solidarity' is a word often regarded with suspicion, as a political word. (The WCC Decade of Churches in Solidarity with Women was renamed 'Count me in!' in this country for this reason.) It is a word which conveys a sense of being with, of being alongside, while not being identical with. In that sense it is an incarnational word: it is a contemporary equivalent of 'Emmanuel – God with us'. It speaks of a God present with, alongside human beings in their suffering. It moves away from the connotations of hierarchy in models of service and rescue to provide a model of pastoral care which is empowering and reciprocal. We give and we receive; we teach and we learn;

we offer our strength and we are vulnerable. We may not fully identify with another's experience – of depression, or abuse, or racism – but we can be alongside, working with them, making connections with our own experience, in solidarity with them, as they struggle for their salvation and liberation.

Images of God healing, offering friendship, mothering, being in solidarity with us may help us to think in terms of power within and in relation. How do we begin to create a liturgy and spirituality that uses these images, that will be a source and inspiration and reflection of our caring? What might such a liturgy and expression of worship look like?

The first principle is that such liturgy must arise out of and address the experiences of our lives. We need liturgy for life, for people, that resonates with experiences of birth or illness or achievement or loss. Pastoral liturgy requires listening, creating something for people, not fitting people into the prepackaged words and formulae of existing forms of service. It may not always be possible or appropriate to create new liturgy for every occasion, and sometimes there is a place for words and symbols made special by tradition and association. There are occasions, however, when attentive listening, and responsive choosing and writing, gives rise to worship which genuinely resonates with the pastoral needs of women.

Such liturgy must take female experience seriously. It needs to recognize female bodily experience – menstruation, sexuality, giving birth, sickness and dying. It must acknowledge these experiences as the source of women's joys and hurts, to be celebrated and mourned as they move through the cycles of their lives. If it is to be authentic, such worship must also recognize the oppression and marginalization which women experience, both in our society and in the Church, and not seek to comfort and soothe, but to empower and liberate. It must reflect images of God and models of pastoral care that are based on mutuality, not a one-sided giving, but a recognition that genuine caring is both giving and receiving, being strong and supportive, but also owning need and vulnerability.

Creating such liturgy is a corporate activity, not writing

by committee, which rarely works, but a creating of liturgy which grows out of human interaction and community. Much liturgy which is sensitive to women's needs is emerging in this way. Such liturgy does not just 'happen': it needs a sense of words and their rhythms, awareness of how symbolism works, a sense of movement and dance, a feeling for music, a responsiveness to visual symbolism and colour. It is when these skills are brought together within a community of friendship and care, with reflection and creativity, that we begin to discover worship and spirituality which is genuinely in touch with women's pastoral needs, gifts, and strengths.

Such liturgy and worship will not always be easy or comfortable. Effective and liberating pastoral care requires a readiness to confront a range of emotion – anger at injustice and violence, self-doubt and despair, fear and courage. If worship is not to fall into the trap of a bland sentimentality that glosses over the realities of women's lives, then it must give space for self-questioning and ambivalence – and the recognition of God's presence there. Sometimes exploring the 'shadow side' of an image or metaphor may take us forward – as in looking at the ambiguities of the image of God as mother. Janet Morley (1988) has argued that when we try to make the female visible in our language and prayers, we discover what else has been left out. Exploring the significance of darkness as well as light, silence as well as words, may lead to new insights about God which ring true with the range and depth of women's experience.

As yet we are only beginning to catch a glimpse of what pastoral liturgy for and by women might look like. Women – as individuals and in groups – are beginning to develop and create worship which addresses their pastoral needs. There is a growing rejection of images of God and models of pastoral care which portray women as helpless victims or passive recipients. There is a growth of liturgical material which affirms women's strength and beauty, and gives expression to the depth of their anger.

When I was asked to write something for my god-daughter's baptism, I wrote a prayer which expressed some of my hopes for a child growing into womanhood. I close with that prayer, because it also gives voice to the hope and possibility that I see as women celebrate their lives in worship, which is liberating and empowering.

## These I Would Bring

If I could bring you
gifts for living in my hand
these I would bring

I would bring the gift of beauty:
not the doll-like definitions of others,
but beauty that springs from within,
flowing from joy in your body and its form.

I would bring the gift of strength;
not the ruthless trampling down of others,
but strength to choose and walk your road
and turn in trust to those around.

I would bring the gift of courage:
not for wild adventure and reckless daring,
but courage to name your hidden fears,
and shine in the clarity of your truth.

I would bring the gift of love:
not for easy comfort or blind dependence,
but love that pulses fiercely within
and finds its strength in tender embrace.

I can bring no gifts but my prayers
reaching into the unknown future:
where the God who shapes and holds you
gives more than words can say.

REFERENCES

Borrowdale, A. (1989). *A Woman's Work: Changing Christian Attitudes*. London, SPCK.

McFague, S. (1987). *Models of God: Theology for an Ecological Nuclear Age*. London, SCM Press.

Morley, J. (1988). *Liturgy and Danger*. In M. Furlong, ed., *Mirror to the Church: Reflections on Sexism*. London, SPCK.

# 16 *Childbirth, Liturgy, and Ritual – A Neglected Dimension of Pastoral Theology*

THELMA ALDCROFT

## *Childbirth and professional power*

The night Sister bustled in, syringe in hand. 'I'm just going to give you an injection', she announced, with scarcely a glance in my direction.

'No, you are not!'

Momentarily startled, she stopped in her tracks and looked at me for the first time. Quickly reasserting her authority she began to rehearse the reasons for having analgesia before the pains became too severe. This was my first baby, and she had knowledge and experience of these things. She continued in her advance, brooking no denial.

'Touch me with that, and I will sue for assault.'

The atmosphere was now hostile.

'You have not even assessed my progress yet!' And then, almost apologetically, 'I am a midwife myself.' I hated myself for that. I didn't want to pull rank, but I was determined to have this baby without any interference. That meant keeping all my faculties alert, not numbed with pain-relief.

My own midwifery training over a quarter of a century ago was greatly influenced by our principal tutor, a declared feminist. She made a practice of sitting in on any lectures given to us by the obstetric consultant, challenging him frequently. The long-running battle between them was such a source of amusement to student midwives over the years that I wonder how many recognized the deadly earnestness of the fight. However, the legacy left by our training was a pride and confidence in our profession.

A few years later, giving birth to our first baby, I had to use all this knowledge and confidence to protect myself and our baby from unnecessary medical intervention. The emotional cost was high but worth it. It also made me realize how difficult it must be for the average woman to stand up against the power of the medical fraternity.

## Pregnancy: process or pathology?

It is accepted that only about fifteen to twenty percent of all labours are unavoidably complicated, and yet there is a national intervention rate of over fifty percent. Much of this depends on the whim of individual obstetricians, with very little evaluation carried out. Consequently caesarian section rates, as an example, can differ from one institution to another, as well as from country to country. In Norway and Holland only three percent of babies are delivered by section, yet the rate in the US has risen to forty percent. England reached a rate of twelve percent in 1986. Rates are also higher among patients receiving private care.

Moving births from home to hospital alters the power structure from the woman to the professionals and from the midwives to the consultant obstetricians, who are powerfully influential in shaping attitudes and hospital policy.

Most women find attendance at hospital antenatal clinics an ordeal. Long waits, often with no facilities for children, accompany impersonal care and sometimes humiliating or frightening examinations. The suggestion is that clinic 'defaulters' risk harming their babies. It is certainly true among this group, but associated factors are also lower: social class, poor housing and nutrition, social deprivation generally and extreme youth. Improvements in social conditions have increased survival rates; although medical intervention has played a part, its importance is often over-estimated.

It is questionable whose interests modern technology serves. Electronic monitoring, for example, plays an important role in defending obstetricians from possible litigation; but for the woman it means being uncomfortably tethered, having the focus of attention shifted from her to the machinery, and impedes close physical contact with her companion.

The recent Commons Health Committee report on maternity services has at last recognized that doctors have turned what should be a natural process into a kind of illness. It comments that there is no evidence that home births are less safe than births in high technology hospital units and that midwives, rather than obstetricians, should have the predominant rôle in the care of pregnant women. 'For the vast majority of pregnant women a successful outcome requires very little in the way of medical care.' (HMSO, 1992)

## Self-Esteem and motherhood

My subsequent experience as both a health visitor and a Relate counsellor would suggest that the consequences of this for women are more than academic, but are rather part of a whole network of constraints which undermine women's self-esteem.

Feelings of anger and violation are not uncommon, particularly when there has been medical intervention in the birth process. However, it is difficult for a woman to admit this, even to herself. Centuries of art and glossy magazines have portrayed motherhood in glamorous terms: smiling, fulfilled, Madonna-like creatures, nursing beautiful, contented babies. The reality is often very different. The baby may scream incessantly and the mother may feel emotionally and physically dreadful. Space and permission to express these feelings is essential, but not always easy in a climate which generally demands thankfulness.

My experience as a Relate counsellor to one or both partners in a relationship has alerted me to the frequency with which they traced the beginnings of their problems to the birth of a child. This 'unfinished business' sometimes went back twenty years or more, causing immense misery. Women with particular needs are those who have suffered sexual abuse during childhood. The whole process of giving birth can reactivate early, painful experiences, not always at a conscious level at the time. There would seem to be an increased potential if there has been a high level of intervention in an otherwise natural process. The inability to express these strong emotions can sometimes lead to depression.

# Childbirth, Liturgy, and Ritual

## Implications for pastoral care

Pastoral support for women following childbirth has always been important, but increasingly so during the last thirty years of increasing technology, bringing its own particular problems. This raises questions about how and by whom pastoral care should be provided. Elaine Graham's (1989) research of twentieth-century pastoral literature relating to women has shown that the needs of women are unlikely to be understood and catered for by a male-dominated church. Clergy were seen as the centre of pastoral action, and preferred not to engage with issues around women's needs, sexuality, or relationship. The twin features of clericalism and sexism emphasized the role of the minister rather than the needs of the client, rendered the pastoral needs of women invisible, and also excluded women as agents or initiators of pastoral care.

Their exclusion from the ordained ministry has left liturgy and ritual, as enacted care, particularly impoverished. Pastoral counselling though invaluable has its limitations. It necessarily remains rooted in one-to-one personal encounter and the realm of the private. A fair degree of verbal articulation is needed, favouring the middle class with their 'elaborated' code of speech, rather than the 'restricted' code of the working class described by Bernstein.

However, ritual transcends both these limitations. It works at a precognitive level, enabling people to enact rather than explain, and moves issues from the private into the public domain: 'The practice of corporate ritual is a function of being human and a proclamation about the social, relational and personal nature of our humanness.' (Grainger, 1988). He continues that Christian ritual is also: 'an entrance to a new kind of life,' and 'the demonstration of the Personhood of God, who is also experienced as being present in the rite.' Grainger is critical of Christians who resent the 'unchurched' using the 'occasional offices'. Negative views act as a barrier to that gateway. Sacramental experience should be available to all in forms that are redemptive, healing, and enlightening. To what extent, therefore, can rituals following childbirth more adequately meet women's pastoral needs?

## Traditional liturgical responses to childbirth

The Church of England has made available 'The Thanksgiving of Women after Childbirth', commonly called 'The Churching of Women' to be found in the 1662 *Book of Common Prayer*. This followed on from the Sarum rite called 'The Purification of a Woman after Childbirth before the Church Porch'. The original intention, as the title suggests, was to purify women from uncleanness after childbirth before attending Mass. She was met at the church porch by the priest, who sprinkled her with Holy Water before leading her into church.

Because the rite belonged to the realm of folk religion, this notion of 'churching' (the popular name for the Office) as a cleansing ritual lived on long after the Church had changed the emphasis to a service for thanksgiving. It was considered unlucky for a new mother to enter someone else's home before she had been churched, and, likewise, older women in particular, would be reluctant to enter her home. I was aware of this belief as a child brought up in Manchester, and was still coming across it as a practising health visitor in Salford up to 1971 when I left the area.

Maurice Staton's (1981) research in Newcastle-upon-Tyne in 1979 showed how the demand for churching had persisted in areas of high female solidarity, in spite of the Church's discomfort and disapproval. Reasons for the demand were vague, but still tended to centre around the old ideas of purification. Newer rites in all denominations have rightly moved away from ideas about uncleanliness, but have also altered the emphasis from the mother to the child. I would suggest that it is important to change this emphasis back to the mother precisely because women are not encouraged to admit that they have needs which are separate from their babies. Valerie Saiving Goldstein (1979) in her demand for a reconsideration of sin and redemption, identified the main sin for women not as pride but as lacking a centre, with little 'self' to sacrifice.

I find it curious that the notion of uncleanness associated with childbirth has persisted for so long among women in spite of the Churches' discouragement. In the area studied by Staton, only eight out of a total of thirty-one women who participated in the rite had understood churching in a way that would be in keeping with present church teaching.

While rejecting entirely the earlier beliefs of the Church that women's biological functions are unclean, I do wonder if at some unconscious and mainly inarticulate level women do recognize that there is some form of cleansing, or, at least, healing, needing to be done. This need, arising from their own experience of childbirth, is unlikely to be understood and catered for by a male-dominated church.

## Reclaiming the liturgy

In recent years, there has been a growing awareness among feminist women of feelings of exclusion and alienation from the Church's worship as the deeply sexist nature of both words and symbols is increasingly recognized. Ruether (1985) argues:

> Women in contemporary churches are suffering from linguistic deprivation and eucharistic famine. They can no longer nurture their souls in alienating words that ignore or systematically deny their existence – they are starved for symbolic forms that fully and wholeheartedly affirm their personhood.

To 'do' theology liturgically, women have formed separatist groups in order to challenge masculine norms of language and symbol, rather than wait for church reform. The growth of circles of community has been a phenomenon of this past decade. A handful of women meeting to form our local group grew to a membership of almost forty in less than two years. The emphasis also seems to be changing from a concern to change the institutional church to simply *being* church.

Excluded from their place in the Anglican ordained ministry, women have created their rituals outside the male-imposed traditions which emphasize hierarchy and separation. Broken circles leave space for others to join, and emphasize community.

Worship is participatory and risks are taken as ideas are explored. The balance between rationality and affectivity is redressed, emphasizing the sacramental in taste, touch, and smell, as well as vision. Bodily movement becomes more possible, and dance is more easily used as an expressive art. Readings may be chosen and shared from a wide variety of sources. Sermons are often replaced by discussion and dialogue: women telling their story, listening to their neighbours' stories and reflecting upon them in the light of the Gospel. The public and the personal are brought more fully together in mutual trust and friendship.

In searching for a suitable liturgy to replace churching, there are two specific considerations to be borne in mind: First, that there should be scope for expressing negative emotions, possibly anger; and second, the emphasis should be on the mother and *her* needs.

## Anger

The expression of anger has become a problem for Christians, and expression in worship has been minimal. Where it does exist, it is usually only as a reflection of Christianity's roots in Judaism, most notably in the Psalms. Attempts have been made to remove even this, by bracketing for exclusion all the 'nasty' verses.

Interestingly, the 1662 service does at least allow some expression of distress through the choice of Psalm 116: 'The snares of death compassed me round about and the pains of hell gat hold of me...I found trouble and heaviness and called upon the name of the Lord. O Lord, I beseech thee deliver my soul.' – but this was dropped from the *Alternative Service Book*.

Monica Furlong (1980) has noted a tendency to drive out darkness, chaos, and fear, and to equate goodness with order, discipline, and control. She argues that this is the wrong approach, and that only by inviting the chaos back into our lives would we realize both the immensity of God, and the goodness within ourselves with our potential for unity, collaboration, and human fullness: 'at the heart of Christian belief, I sense an awareness that chaos is not to be shut out and ignored; that on the contrary it may be the specific task of the christian, or at least of those whom we call holy, to explore, confront, become conscious of, perhaps even befriend, chaos.'

These elements are missing from modern conservative liturgical material and from feminist rituals of thanksgiving for the birth of a child. However, women's experience of brokenness, abuse, and rape is well represented in many feminist healing rituals and could be used, where appropriate, within a childbirth ritual.

Rosemary Radford Ruether argues that it is not easy to separate rites of healing from life-cycle rites, since acts of violence and the need for healing from violence occur so frequently in many women's lives. However, the connection between more overt kinds of violence and more subtle forms carried out in the name of medical science does not appear to have been made.

## The Needs of the mother

The other requirement – that of finding a ritual which focuses on the mother, rather than the child – presents more of a problem. There is no shortage of imagery in prayers and readings of nurturing womb, labouring, and giving birth, but a ritual in which a woman was able to relive and reclaim the process of actually giving birth does not appear to exist, even in places where it claimed to do so! Feminist life-cycle rituals jump from antenatal rituals to rituals surrounding the baby. As women are always discovering, the anticipation and the reality can be very far apart.

This surprising silence even from feminist liturgists reflects accurately the feelings expressed by women at the postnatal support groups I convene. Throughout the pregnancy they are the focus of attention, but as soon as the baby is born they are discarded like empty containers, and attention shifts rapidly to the baby, leaving them feeling like nonpersons. This feeling was neatly summed up by one of the group, who worked in the evening as a barmaid. She dearly loves her children, but is struggling to hold on to her identity: 'Before the children were born, the fellers used to say "Hi, Angela. How are you?" Now they say, "Hi, Angela. How are the kids?" It's as if I've ceased to exist as a person in my own right.'

While thinking around the possibilities of constructing a

ritual which redressed the balance in favour of the mother (the child has its own naming rituals, or baptism) I was struck by another realization. I was musing on how women express their pains and fears, as well as their thanks, in the supportive company of other women. This is just as true within worship, when given the chance, as it is over a cup of coffee. On special occasions, our Women in Theology group has set aside time for healing space within our worship. It is very unlike traditional healing services within the Church, when wounds are nursed in silent privacy, then taken to the priest or minister at the altar rail for God's healing. In our women's circles we share our pain, reflect upon it, laugh and cry together, and possibly anoint each other.

## Liturgy affirming women's experiences

Within that kind of supportive framework a newly delivered woman could be given space and permission to talk about the birth, how it actually was for her, and the feelings that are left surrounding it. If it has been a joyous and fulfilling occasion, then all can rejoice with her. If not, then there can be opportunity to express the hurt, and healing space can be given, before passing on to thanksgiving. Other women who have already had the experience of giving birth can perhaps briefly outline how it has been for them, as a way of enabling and giving permission to speak.

It is fairly well known that most women remember almost every intimate detail of their labours and births if anyone troubles to ask them. The experience appears to behave like suppressed material, unfinished business, endlessly reasserting itself with emotional vividness. Perhaps this is because women are not given the space when they need it most, soon after the delivery. Perhaps its omission from feminist celebrations is a further reflection of this, possibly a collective repression resulting from the centuries of male-imposed taboo. If this is the case, then an adequate ritual becomes even more essential to enable women to bring the experience to full consciousness. I have already noted that women who have been previously sexually abused may have particular needs, but many other women also need to be able to give expression to deep feelings which may be present. This may include anger and other powerful emotions which they may have been taught are unacceptable, as well as thanksgiving. Medical intervention may increase feelings of violation.

## Liturgy and conflict

Any ritual celebrating childbirth needs to be worked out and tried within the confines of what Ruether terms 'Women Church'. Essentially, it is mothers' experience alone which will shape it, though that need not exclude partners from its eventual enactment. That choice will depend on the needs of the woman and may not be too difficult if the birth has been straightforward. Those women for whom the unfinished business of previous sexual abuse has been opened up, or those who have felt violated by the birth process in other ways, may need a gathered congregation of women only. Such groups are now to be found in most major cities within various organizations, such as Women in Theology, Women Space, and Well Woman liturgical groups in some university chaplaincies.

A decision will have to be made about whether inclusive or specifically feminine language and symbolism should be used. A friend who is a conservative Christian in the Anglo-Catholic tradition, once said to me, 'Refering to God as "She" actually makes some women feel physically sick.' I do not doubt her. My professional experiences have shown me how deeply runs the revulsion some women have towards their own bodies. There are women who can't look at, let alone touch, their own genital areas, women who have passed this revulsion on, mothers to daughters. Images planted by the early Church fathers who equated the female with the 'lower order' of nature, sex, pollution, sin, and death, have bitten deeply into women's psychological make-up. As a consequence, it is difficult for women to believe deeply in their own sacredness and capacity to image the Divine.

Kathleen Fischer (1989) has described what happens when abused women in particular are invited to image God as female:

189

She was behind me
She seemed small
She would not come forward
She kept her head down
She would not speak
I asked her again to come to me but she couldn't.

## Liturgy and Darkness

Janet Morley (1988) notes that when it comes to confronting the dark side of God it is all too easy for women to identify God exclusively with the forces of patriarchy and dominance: 'If I can distance Him as wholly "Other" just as men and men's systems are wholly "other" to me, I can afford to fight. How can I bear it if it is "She" who tolerates such suffering, "She" in whose image I am made, "She" who is closer to me than my body, "She" who should understand?' Morley goes on to make the point that it is not only images of God which may be changed but also images of women: 'And so devising new liturgies as women is dangerous because it risks exposing conflict...one of the temptations for feminists is to speak as if women possessed a sort of primal innocence that be recovered by escaping from male-dominated forms of thought and language.'

Imaging God as She exposes us not only to the dark side of God but the dark side of ourselves as well. This dark side, which women find in the process of giving birth, needs to be articulated, and women given space and permission to do so. It needs to be done urgently and not only verbally. To reach to the deeper depths of our being, it needs to be enacted in liturgy and symbol.

That night we gathered for the birth, as women
have always done – as women
have never done till now;
and in an ordinary room,
warm, exposed, and intimate as childbed,
we spoke about our bodies and our blood,
waiting for God's delivery:
silence, gesture and speech
announcing, with a strange appropriate blend

*Childbirth, Liturgy, and Ritual*

of mystery and bluntness,
the celebration of the word made flesh
midwived wholly by women. (Morley, 1992)

The potential this kind of worship offers is a source of empowerment for women, and for the Church; a theological and pastoral education.

REFERENCES
Fischer, K. (1989). *Women at the Well*. London, SPCK.
Furlong, M. (1980). 'Afraid of the Dark'. *Church Times*. 22 February.
Grainger, R. (1988). *The Message of the Rite*. London, Lutterworth Press.
Graham, E. (1989). 'The Pastoral Needs of Women'. *Contact* 1989:3.
HMSO (1992). Maternity Services, Health Committee, vol. 1. Quoted in *The Guardian*, 5 March 1992.
Morley, J. (1988). 'Liturgy and Danger'. In M. Furlong, ed., *Mirror to the Church*. London, SPCK.
Morley, J. (1992). *All Desires Known*. London, SPCK.
Saiving (Goldstein), V. (1979). 'The Human Situation: A Feminine View'. In C. P. Christ and J. Plaskow, eds, *Womanspirit Rising: A Feminist Reader in Religion*. New York, Harper & Row.
Staton, M. (1981). 'Churching – Past and Present'. *Contact* 1981:3.
Ruether, R. (1985). *Women-Church: Theology and Practice of Feminist Liturgical Communities*. San Francisco, Harper & Row.

# 17 *Breaking Open the Bible*

## HEATHER WALTON

I walk through the streets of Moss Side. On a clear, sunny day you can see the moors rising in the distance from the bottom of Claremont Road. A little Asian girl in a purple silk party dress and Day-Glo pink tights nearly knocks me over with her tricycle. It is warm, but the prostitutes wear coats over their underwear. Two older women stand talking, their shopping trollies parked respectable and erect beside them. Young girls are pregnant; middle-aged women pushing grandchildren are pregnant. Posters hang tattered from the hoardings on burnt-out buildings. 'Fly Direct to New York'. Not as silly as it sounds: we are a travelling population – women left children in the Caribbean when they came here, and now have grandchildren in London, Kingston, and Chicago.

In our little village life teems and rages while the sun shines and the hills rise purple against the horizon. The striking patterns of women's lives glow in the sunlight. They are vivid. It is hard to notice the pale shades of the Christian story. The colours have faded, and I am not even sure I want to strain to see them. There is a lot here to occupy the eyes, the mind, and heart and soul.

Much has been made in recent years of our shift in understanding about what theology is. Many would now prefer to replace the equation 'theology is God-talk' with 'theology is God-story', implying that our faith is not propositional but narrative, that we are telling a story of God's involvement in our experience rather than making philosophical universal truth claims. Clearly, Scripture is God-story, and even doctrine, it is claimed, is story. It has an obscured narrative, a metaphorical past. The whole of theology is narrative through and through – but the foundational narratives of Scripture will be my special concern here.

I suspect many women are quite at ease and happy with

the current reassessment of the power of narrative. Women's culture is story-rich and powerfully imaginative, and many of us would gladly acknowledge the force of narratives to inspire, to challenge, and to change. However, we have a major problem with the foundational stories of the Christian faith. In many of them, women are marginal and casually despised. Certainly our concerns and our achievements lie buried beneath the thick varnish of the male editor's hand. Even in the present day, a male guild of biblical scholars carefully guard access to scriptural knowledge. So how can the Bible be any help to women in our theological reflection and pastoral practice?

When we have disturbing thoughts like these there are always those who rush in eager to comfort us: Praise be to God, we are reminded, the Christian tradition contains many stories. Some of these are undoubtedly hostile to women, but if concubines are mutilated and daughters offered as sacrifice to the King of Heaven, then do not forget that on other pages women have dignity, power and a certain place within the Kingdom. All we must do is to be careful about the stories we choose – some will be helpful, and others not.

But perhaps we do not even need to be so exclusive. Is not the work of biblical exegesis and historical reconstruction a way of retelling the story so that our communities may see the true relevance of the narratives for our own time? Although few in number, there are women biblical scholars like Phyllis Trible (1979), for example, who challenge the assumptions brought to the exegesis of biblical narratives. In her scholarly opinion, even a narrative like that of Adam and Eve can be reclaimed for it does not describe woman as a secondary creature ordained to serve man. Adham, the original human, is ungendered; both maleness and femaleness being later characteristics and neither superior to the other.

Similarly, historical theologians like Elizabeth Fiorenza (1983) help us to see behind biblical texts. Her studies of the earliest Christian communities enable us to trace how the contribution of women was systematically edited out of the Christian story. Nevertheless, traces of the powerful women in the primitive church remain, and from these we can begin to redraw the pictures of women which have been excluded from the biblical documents; we can begin to tell new stories 'in memory of her'.

It is important that we recognize what is happening in these processes of historical reconstruction and feminist exegesis. We are in fact bringing something to the text which it does not contain in order that its impact and relevance might become clearer. In doing so, we are really creating new stories that can function for us with greater power, but at the same time we are retaining an obvious and authentic connection with the past. This is in fact a process which Christians have always engaged in, and is the one which currently holds sway in theological colleges and universities via the historical critical method. However, within it lies a major dilemma.

In order to reach the new 'woman-friendly' version of the old story you have to go back to the ancient text, and it is the ancient text which has the principal status; exegesis and reconstruction remain secondary. It is as if women were issuing a supplement to the Bible and saying to their sisters, 'If you read the Bible with this in your other hand, it will mitigate the text's misogyny'. But the majority who read the Bible aren't protected in this way. They don't labour on Trible's exegetical threshing-floor, separating the reclaimable grain from the chaff of male interpretation. Nor do they take Fiorenza's sieve to the biblical haystack in order to discover a precious past that has been lost. For the majority of women, the Bible remains a powerfully dangerous resource.

It is suggested there may be a way out of even this difficult impasse. Some narrative theologians would assert that the important thing about the biblical stories is not their content but the framework they provide for exploring our own experiences: the stories should not be seen as historical, but paradigmatic of human journeys endlessly repeated and eternally relevant. A woman experiencing the joy of maternal creativity would find a home for her celebration in the framework of the Lucan nativity story. A woman experiencing the pain of self-awareness and seeking freedom might resonate with the Exodus story, although in my experience women seem to try to identify first with the Abrahamic legends and all the confusing messages and bleak images they contain.

In this vein, Rosemary Ruether (1983) has encouraged woman to identify a prophetic scriptural trajectory in which our quest for freedom and equality can be located. It could be argued that such is the depth and power of the God story we tell based upon Scripture that 'the whole of human life is there', and each woman's struggles and aspirations can somehow find their home inserted into a scriptural framework.

But still I am uneasy. I am uneasy because all the approaches I have so far mentioned are anxious to fit the living woman to the text. This is done either by choosing a story that superficially seems to correspond to our experience; or by stretching the story to fit by exegesis or reconstruction, which, as we have seen, is to make a supplementary story; or by simply inserting the woman piecemeal into a biblical framework through which she will tell her story. But what if the stories from the store of faith are simply inadequate vehicles to convey a woman's experience of rape, infertility, or loving other women, for example? What if the world of our experiences cannot happily be clothed with an existing Christian narrative, or enclosed within a scriptural framework? What then?

In a short paper, Rowan Williams (1989) highlights the issue for me:

> The Church may be committed to interpreting the world in terms of its own foundational narratives; but the very act of interpreting *affects the narratives as well as the world*...and is not restricted to what we usually think of as the theological mainstream.' (My emphasis.)

For women, then, the encounter between the reality of our lives and the foundational stories of the Christian tradition must become a generative act, a moment of conception which does not leave the stories unchanged anymore than it leaves us unchanged. The Bible stories must not become the dead husks of orthodoxy; they must must crack open to

reveal the seeds which they contain. And it is their seeds
which matter, not the shells, for from them will grow new
narratives which resonate with our lived experience. For
Williams this 'splitting open' of our stories is always
prompted by encounter with others and through our experience of the world. So it is not now any more a question of
inserting women's experience into a scriptural framework,
but creating a new story out of our dialogue with women's
lives. This can happen in at least two ways.

First, through hearing the narratives of others. The novel-
ist Jean Rhys wrote a powerful short story entitled, *La
Gross Fifi*. In it, the narrator is a young woman, in desperate
misery over what we do not know, stuck in a seedy hotel.
Another of the occupants is Fifi, a fat, fifty-year-old woman,
and her gigolo. Friends warn the narrator to shift hotels, to
move away from the corrupting influence of this ageing
degenerate. But it is in Fifi's presence, and through her
accepting kindness that the young woman begins to find
some relief. Fifi's love is passionate, generous, bodily,
common, accepting. The young woman comes to care deeply
for her, and to observe her giving of herself to the worthless
gigolo because she cannot help herself: she has got to have
him. For all that, Fifi's love is generous; it is jealous. Her
tale is tragic: she is stabbed to death by her lover in a
passionate quarrel, but her presence survives this violent
end, and continues to nourish the narrator on her road into
the future. Fifi is not simply dead.

This is a story of love, but about love of a kind which our
foundational narratives know nothing. Immoral, physical,
tragic – and yet potentially healing, redemptive. We hear in
it the possibility of a different story of God. God loves
humanity as Fifi loves her gigolo, passionately, wilfully,
physically. God loves humanity as some women love. Not
caring too much about the morality of it, but enjoying the
sex, admiring the style, making herself ridiculous. Even
worse, we hear a story of God loving when love destroys
both herself and others. We hear a story of a God who is
killed because of love; not to balance some eternal scales of
good and evil, but because killing and dying are part of
love. But, ah, we rise again – we rise again!

I tell Fifi's story because it is paradigmatic of a very different loving to that celebrated in the biblical stories. It is, however, a kind of loving women know well – albeit one that remains scandalous and very difficult for feminists to name. This is the sort of loving that cannot be slotted willy-nilly into our foundational narratives; some new creating must take place.

To describe such experiences of loving, we must tell stories that are not told. This is a great challenge for the Christian preacher or theologian in living touch with the tradition, but aware that the tradition has new space for stories such as these. Then the tradition must be split apart to reveal its seeds. There is an urgent need to create new stories of God which allow God to speak to us afresh. Telling Fifi's story alongside the tale of the Crucifixion changes both.

Second, in our dialogue with women's experience, new stories are born when we recognize scandals in our foundational narratives to which familiarity has blinded us previously. New stories are born when we refuse to run away from these scandals, but instead explore them and let them challenge us. Rowan Williams again reminds us of the work that must be done by believers in boundary contexts, and particularly by Christian feminists:

> The Christian at the frontier of politics or science will frequently find that he or she *will not know what to say.* There can be a real loss in respect to traditional formulae not because they are being translated but because they are being tested....The Christian woman actively involved in feminism will record the same kind of tension. The paradox of our situation often seems to be...that integrity in preaching leads us close to those who least tolerate some aspects of that teaching. (Williams, 1989)

In other words, our foundational stories may look pretty unhelpful to our feminist women friends, and unsuitable for them in satisfying pastoral need. So what do we do? Often what we do is we don't tell them to women in distress or to women seeking liberation – we keep them for church. I am frequently asked by intrigued feminist friends, 'Can I come and hear you preach?' My heart fills with fear. But this embarrassing pressure has helped me to notice the scandal of the biblical texts, and now I preach about Rachel weeping for her children and she cannot be comforted, rather than the little baby Messiah sleeping his way to Egypt. I preach Hagar and Sarah, not Abraham, and new stories are being born. There is no scriptural mandate for them, their place in the Christian tradition is problematic to say the least. But they are being born anyway – and need to be.

I walk through the streets of Moss Side and a thousand-and-one women's stories leap to heart and mind and soul. Some are easily linked by my scriptural imagination to the precious stories of tradition. Others are not, but still demand their place within a developing Christian pastoral narrative. They are stories relevant to us, owned by us, and useful to us, and they must be told. It must be admitted, however, that this is not a process that can take place without misgivings among believers hesitant to tamper with tradition. Nevertheless, we must be brave and create, remembering what has taken place before.

Most scholars now agree that the current ending of Mark's Gospel is a later addition contrived by editors who were discontented with the way the story was originally told. Similarly, John's Gospel was the subject of much controversy and only just found its way into the Canon. People were shocked to hear the story of God's revelation in Christ told in what was for them a radical, shocking, and possibly heretical form. It should give us confidence to know that Christians have battled about who tells the story in what way and for what purpose through the centuries. This time, women's voices must be heard.

REFERENCES

Fiorenza, E.S. (1983). *In Memory of Her: A Feminist Theological Reconstruction of Christian Origins*. London, SCM Press.
Ruether, R.R. (1983). *Sexism and God-Talk*. London, SCM Press.
Trible, P. (1979). 'Eve and Adam: Genesis 2–3 Reread'. In C.P. Christ and J. Plaskow, eds, *Womanspirit Rising: A Feminist Reader in*

*Religion*. New York, Harper & Row.

Williams, R.D. (1989). 'Postmodern Theology and the Judgement of the World'. In F. Burnham, ed., *Postmodern Theology: Christian Faith in a Pluralist World*. San Francisco, Harper & Row.

# 18 *Women and Ministerial Training*

SUSAN F. PARSONS

I have just spent an hour in my office with a woman who is beginning after one year in training to feel anxious about her future in the Church. We talk about her sense of obligation to God, and of her commitment to serve the Church, and she expresses her willingness to go forward to meet the Church's call for her ministry. However, already something unseen yet powerful is drawing her attention away from this clear vision, causing her to ask questions of herself, her motives, her self-image, and of her understanding of God – questions which are unsettling, and which challenge her faith at its deepest level. She is beginning to feel the impact of the unwritten code of acceptability within the ministry, and to sense the pressure to succumb or to run.

This piece arises out of my work as an administrator and tutor on a ministerial training course. The course includes both lay people and ordinands from a variety of denominations. Half of the students are women, and half of those are training as ordinands. I wish to highlight one kind of experience women may have in the process of training for ministry; to analyse some aspects of the structural reinforcement of this experience; and to offer a brief theological reflection related to women and pastoral care.

## Experience

The people who come to the course are 'mature', that is, they are all over the age of thirty (this is the only essential criterion for admission), and thus they each have a wide range of personal, family, and work experience. A study of incoming students' application forms indicates there is no difference between the genders in educational or technical and professional qualifications, except at degree level, where there are only slightly more men than women with degrees. Some indication of the things they have done is discovered at our initial interview, during which applicants tell about their jobs; the training they have had in their chosen field; the kinds of skills they normally use; and the talents which they propose to bring to the practice of ministry. In many cases they are men and women with responsible positions at work or in the Church, and have a range of skills at their disposal, which they seek to develop and use in a new way. In other cases they may not have had a great deal of paid work experience, or may not have been in positions of authority, but have had some educational background and life experience that is relevant.

## A question of confidence

What interests me at interview stage and in the early days of the course is the confidence the men and women reveal: they are enthusiastic to participate as fully as possible, encouraged by what the course may offer, and committed to deriving the fullest benefit from the training. Certainly doubts are expressed in some form about what they will actually be doing in the churches, and they have not all had encouragement from their home churches/parishes in considering a form of ministry. Indeed, some have had rather painful experiences in discerning and testing their vocation to ordination. But on the whole they believe in themselves, and we are pleased to reinforce that positive attitude.

What happens in training is something that is almost imperceptible, but none the less tangible in its end result, namely that women ordinands leave the course with a confidence 'problem', while men either do not have this 'problem', or it is heavily masked. The evidence for this comes from the final-year Practical Ministry Placement, which is carried out during the third term of that year, just as the students finish their training. It is a skill-centred placement. Students are asked to identify the range of skills they expect to be exercising during their future ministries, to consider especially those which are not yet so well developed, and to focus the placement on practising those under-developed skills with a specialist. In assessing the placement, the student, the supervisor/host, and the chaplain, who is a local tutor, each complete a form answering various questions regarding the development of skills, strengths, and weaknesses of the student's practice that were obvious on placement, and expectations for future training needs. It is at this point that the disparity between men and women becomes clear.

It is said of women candidates in particular that the placement has primarily served to develop their confidence, or to overcome feelings of inferiority, or to help them discover a belief in their own abilities. It is said that the placement has been a good experience in this regard: a woman who lacked self-confidence now has some, a woman who did not believe in herself now does so. Thus, many women answer the question, 'What do you value most about your performance on placement?' by saying, 'The confidence I gained'. In answer to the question regarding observed weaknesses in ministry evident in the placement, many supervisors report the 'need to believe in her strengths', or 'would grow in confidence with more experience'. Women themselves report this about their experience, and others say it about them – Methodist, Anglican, URC alike. This is not something that appears in the assessment forms about men, and they themselves do not report it as a matter of interest or concern. It also is generally not something that appears either in the assessment forms about lay people who have been exploring various contributions they might make to the life and mission of the churches. What has happened?

## Analysis

How is it that men and women can come through the training experience with such different attitudes towards themselves, and beliefs about their work within the Church? Why is the matter of confidence raised for women but not for men? There are many factors we might take into account: personality differences, family background and circumstances, available role models, the content and style of the training experience, and so on. Here, I will focus only on one factor, namely the influence of the institutional church on this moment in the preparation of its ministers. It is my belief that the experience of the institution and of its unwritten codes influences profoundly the nature of the training experience; conditions one's consciousness in a particular way; and shapes the pastoral problems and opportunities for women who enter the ordained ministry.

AN INSTITUTIONAL PROBLEM

Three features of institutional structure can be highlighted in this analysis: first, authority is transferable for men in a way that it is not for women; second, there are not the same possibilities for the exercise of ministry for men and for women; third, the descriptions and expectations of ministry differ along gender-specific lines. I call these things 'structural' because they are not the particular responsibility of individuals, but are characteristic features of the structures of the churches, patterns of authority which operate within them, and descriptions of the roles which the churches recognize and accredit.

The first point suggests there is a link between the exercise of authority and the presence of previous skills and experience that are transferred to a new role. On the whole, this is an easier transition for men than for women. It is assumed that men who have been teachers, managers in business or industry, lawyers, social workers, and so on will be able to transfer the skills they have used in one field to their new rôle within the Church. They are encouraged to expect this, to assume a welcome reception by the Church, to believe their colleagues will happily embrace their skills and experience, and to anticipate a mere sideways step from one institutional setting to another. Men report to me after training the affirmation and respect they have received, and the relative ease with which another mantle has been taken up. If this creates a problem for them, it is likely to be in remaining at their place of work, where, as ministers in secular employment, their loyalty and allegiance to their employers may be questioned. This suggests that even in the larger society there is an expectation of ministerial authority upon men that may rest

*Changing Lives*

uneasily with other career developments; but the exercising of this authority is not on the whole a problem for them within the churches.

This is not so for women, who by contrast experience de-skilling. Women learn the meaning of being under authority rather than how to exercise it. The justification of this belief is that after all ministry – for women – is about service, while for men it is about the assumption and exercise of authority. Because women are not expected to hold or carry authority in the same way as men within the ministry, a double standard emerges in which gender is the deciding factor.

One incumbent complained that a woman ordinand from his parish 'did not know the meaning of service'; another protested that while a woman may have had some prominence in her former job, she is 'only a junior deacon here'. Women who come forward, asking recognition of their former selves are considered threatening. They may either bear this in silent suffering, or become angry. A woman is considered ready for ministry when she is able to put her husband's interests ahead of her own and give them higher priority, for she will then understand the nature of serving others. Those who make decisions in the same free and responsible way as previously are challenged, and asked to submit to others' judgments. It is not unknown for women's thoughtful decisions in ministry to be changed or overruled by men in higher positions. Those who enthusiastically bring their previous expertise to bear on a new issue are quietened or given tasks they may not understand or do so well. In one sense this might be a transitional matter while the Church adjusts itself to changes in other social institutions, but this does not wholly explain the invisible wall women meet when they attempt to come into ministry as equals.

A second feature of the institutional church that encourages the confidence 'problem' is the lack of posts for women, resulting in a structural inability to exercise their calling. Each autumn, a pile of parish profiles accumulates on my desk from dioceses with vacancies for deacons. Whereas the pile with vacancies for male deacons needs a

204

paperweight to hold it down, the vacancies for women deacons are easily memorized. There are women who are free for stipendiary ministry, but no posts are available. Thus there are high numbers of reluctant or unwilling non-stipendiary ministers among women, and the consequent costs of their unpaid work are borne and given freely to the church by hardworking husbands and families. It is no longer plausible that the reason for more women NSMs is because women are unable to move for domestic reasons – and certainly women from this course have gone quite far afield to find stipendiary posts. The problem will most likely intensify with the increasing financial crisis within the Church as it begins to cut back on the number of such positions altogether. In the meantime, the situation re-inforces the use of women in voluntary capacities to perform important services for institutions, without which the structures could not be maintained.

Descriptions of ministry and of pastoral care are often understood within the churches along gender-specific lines. Sometimes this takes the form of crude biological deter-minism, a belief that women's and men's bodies are fit for different kinds of tasks. Women's bodies, being basically nurturing, are naturally attuned to care for the dependent, to act in ways beyond their own self-interest. This belief affirms their unique pastoral sensitivity, their empathy for others' needs, and their altruism, which is learned through the experiences of childbearing and rearing. One woman is welcomed into her new parish with an anticipation of the gentle and kindly touch she will bring to ministry; another is 'useful' for the way in which she soaks up the emotional stress and pain of parishioners; another is valued for being caring without being 'too emotional'; yet another is critic-ized for not being 'pastoral'.

Beyond the obvious point that not all women are alike, the belief that there is a predetermined mould into which we are to be fitted is questionable in biological as well as theological terms. It is important to notice the constraining influence which these stereotypes have upon both women and men, and to recognize that they express the ideological justification for a particular kind of social organization.

Women who do not fit these preconceived expectations, who question existing social organization, whose vision may be prophetic, will have a confidence "problem" in relating to the structures supporting these stereotypes.

## Reflection

The structural factors that influence men and women in their training for ministry thus shapes the understanding and exercising of pastoral care. Here is an instance of an institutional reality shaping personal awareness, and then blaming – in the case of women – or praising – in the case of men – the person for these feelings and beliefs. In order to address the issue seriously for women, attention must not only be directed towards her sense of inadequacy and of sorrow, but must also heighten a critical awareness of the institutional framework that constrains her work.

While both men and women are being confirmed and moulded into the structural requirements for the exercise of their skills and their practice of ministry, they are trained to expect and handle authority in different ways, and their emotional lives and moral characters are shaped differently. Within a structure built upon a double standard of behaviour, which differentially assigns to men and women places of significance within it, it is essential that pastoral care be entangled with issues of justice. In the one example presented we can find an instance of the institution shaping the individuals it requires in fundamentally unequal ways, so that their future work together as partners in ministry is impaired.

Women who do not have a confidence 'problem' learn to look over their shoulders in case a man with a more objective and critical mind is listening; women who have struggled to believe in themselves look for an appointment in which that fragile development will be upheld; women who have ordered their lives and decisions carefully anticipate continuous wrestling with male colleagues, whom they often correctly judge to be less competent; women whose skills are administrative and executive feel self-conscious about exercising these, and guilty about not matching the Church's expectations of them. In these and in many other ways women inculcate the double message of the Church. It is important to know that in women's exercise of pastoral care they may be carrying this encounter with them, and that they have learned a particular kind of 'humility' in response to the structures of the Church.

Women spend time contemplating what they are up against in the churches, what the implications of this weight of power and tradition might be, and whether they have the resources to handle it all. The answers require a lot of personal energy – to draw together the full resources of their personalities; to discover their courage, patience, endurance, and humour; to develop their individual strengths in order to cope with institutional realities. Once again, the imbalance is plain: men find themselves confirmed and strengthened in their roles, since these represent the full leadership roles the Church emphasizes and rewards at its forefront; but the institution requires a different quality of individual commitment and personal strength from women, whom it will not reward or reinforce in the same way. And since the kind of ministry that women bring to the churches is often understood to be the very essence of what ministry is all about – service – this brings a tremendous moral pressure to bear on the practice of it. Dare any woman admit to being weak?

In the midst of all this, women are seeking to describe an ecclesiology which will provide the framework for their exercise of pastoral care. There are at least three alternative theological positions women have taken up: first, that the Church will remain committed to the notion of complementarity, in which different roles will be appropriate for men and for women; second, the Church will move towards offering the same ministerial roles and expectations for men and women; third, women will conceive a new vision for the Church which has not yet been institutionally realized or accepted. Each of these positions will have different implications for women's exercise of pastoral care, and examples of each are currently to be found.

In the first, the unique gifts of women to the Church will be emphasized. Their perspective on spiritual matters, which expresses and reflects a particular embodiment will be encouraged. Their place alongside men who are quite different to themselves will be enjoyed. This expresses a theological anthropology built upon the complementarity of the genders. A key feature of our creation as human beings is that we are given by the creator different responsibilities which are understood to be fundamental to the creator's intentions for full human community. The hope, therefore, is that in being fully themselves as men and as women, a more balanced, total community will result in which both kinds of possibilities for human life are presented through differing gender roles. The Church is thus to be the order of creation fulfilled.

In the second, men and women will be encouraged to discover the qualities of the other gender within themselves. Men thus need to become carers, to discover their own capacity for empathy and altruism, to express and enjoy their emotional and tender natures. Women need to become leaders, to learn how to be authoritative and to exercise authority over others, to make use of their skills in management and decision-making. Some role-reversal is called for. This suggests a different theological anthropology, in which each person is to incorporate their opposite, alter-ego within themselves so that each becomes whole or complete. In the course of this, each person may develop unexpected potential, resulting in more balanced individuals, who express the fullness of human possibilities in their own persons. The Church is then to be a community of disciples faithful to the call to be whole.

In the third, women propose new forms of community altogether, and set out to discover, establish, or encourage these wherever they may be found. Much involvement in sector ministries, in 'unofficial' lay work, in voluntary capacities, means that women are affirming the value of communities outside the Church, and of ways in which people are working together positively without those structural impediments. AIDS self-help groups, day-care and community centres, Asian women's projects, educational groups in prisons, women's refuges, and so on, all embody a hope for communitas not always found in the Church itself. This kind of pastoral care speaks from outside the boundaries of the Church's possibilities, and offers hope for its regeneration. It affirms a view of humanness that seeks to live beyond dualisms, within the recognition of a plurality of forms of life and of personal identity which the language of gender fails altogether to capture. The Church here becomes an eschatological sign of what God has done in the new creation.

In anticipation of the eschaton, women will not respond to pastoral care or become pastoral carers in stereotypical or predictable ways. It is important for us not to generalize about their responses or choices. Women will discover their own integrity in determining appropriate ways of ministering within the framework of their theological convictions regarding the nature of church and of humanness. They will disagree among themselves about these matters. They will engage with others in the ongoing debate about these concerns, which are far from resolved in any sector of society. They will discover in the course of dialogue with and encouragement of each other what the special purpose and meaning of their lives may be. Those churches that either fear or constrain this creative potential, do so to their own impoverishment.

# 19 *The Sexual Politics of Pastoral Care*

### ELAINE L. GRAHAM

How can women and men present a vision of human wholeness – a vision rooted in both Christian tradition and contemporary experience – which will help in the ecumenical task of renewing the Church? The Community study was – and is – at the heart of the ecumenical agenda. It reflects the realization that the world will come to believe not because of the clarity of our doctrinal formulations (important as this is), but because of the quality of our life as a loving, reconciling inclusive community in Christ. (Crawford and Kinnamon, 1983)

## The social context of pastoral care

Attention to the novelty of women as agents and recipients of pastoral care is a matter which goes far beyond the mere process of 'adding in' a new constituency of pastoral ministers and clients to conventional models. Instead, it requires the Church to consider the nature of the core values at the heart of pastoral practice, and the implicit truth-claims of the Christian community as enacted and embodied in diverse patterns of pastoral ministry.

The maxim that 'the personal is political' is a familiar watchword in feminist circles. In recent years, such a claim has also come to prominence in much of the pastoral care literature, with respect to a growing awareness that relations between individuals cannot be immune from the dynamics of a wider network of social relations. Pastoral care literature is beginning to recognize that many of the problems and pressures faced by those who seek help are more than the sum of individual failings, bad decisions, or personal moral culpability. Rather, pastoral carers must be sensitive to the social causes of health and illness; the influence of

cultural norms and the dynamics of family life in the formation of individual personality; and the structural aspects of
public policy and socioeconomic change which act to influence personal circumstances. Such a sensibility is reflected
in speculations that pastoral strategy may involve attention
to social change and political intervention, and not just to
individual amelioration and adjustment. Such an understanding of the politics of pastoral care is beginning to be
widely recognized, and is increasingly informing work which
attends to the development of a pastoral care of women.

However, there is a second dimension to the politics of
pastoral care, distinct from the factors which condition
pastoral need, and which concerns the actual dynamics of
the pastoral care relationship itself. At the heart of every
pastoral encounter are unspoken values about the conduct
of that relationship and the aims and objectives to which
pastoral practice is directed. In a fundamental sense, pastoral care is informed by ideals. It can never be the neutral
carrier of uncontested or value-free objectives which are
simply transacted between agent and client. Embodied in
the apparently straightforward and uncontroversially benign tasks of pastoral care – classically defined as acts of
healing, guiding, reconciling, and sustaining – are assumptions concerning the nature of Christian faith and human
destiny, patterns of authority in the Church, and the very
character of God at work in the world.

Attention to the *politics* of pastoral care, therefore,
begins with the realization that pastoral relationships cannot be isolated from their broader social and cultural
setting, whether this be the political and structural causes
of human need, or the extent to which culture shapes the
values by which women and men live. This may not be
immediately apparent to us, but a consideration of how
such principles vary between historical epochs and cultures
illustrates the strength of societal norms upon the Christian
community's articulation of its own core values.

## Symbols and metaphors of pastoral care

One of the most enduring images in the history of Christian
pastoral care is that of the pastor as shepherd: courageous,

charismatic, and solicitous. Yet increasingly, contemporary voices have spoken of their reservations at such an heroic model, which to present-day tastes appears authoritarian and paternalistic. The emphasis in many quarters of the Church today on the egalitarian nature of the Christian community and the priesthood of all believers is regarded as a reappropriation of such themes of mutuality and inclusiveness in surviving accounts of the early Church. Yet this does not sit well with the implicitly individualistic and undemocratic portrayal of pastoral ministry and Christian vocation embodied in the shepherd. If the pastor is the shepherd, it is argued, then it is unavoidable to think of the congregation or parish as sheep; hardly flattering or empowering!

As with many of the symbols and metaphors of the Christian tradition – forged in a social and cultural context and deploying concepts now foreign – the debate rages as to the possibilities of retrieving such imagery. Here, pastoral theologians are divided, some arguing that the shepherd is such a central icon of Christian pastoral ministry as to impel the contemporary Church to reclaim the model. Such discussions choose to emphasize the courage, unconventionality, and tenacity of the pastor. However, as with the debate on more obvious forms of exclusive language in theology – as, for example, the predominant image of God as Father – it is also argued that such metaphors are not merely sets of words, but reflect and perpetuate particular world views and ideologies. In other words, the preferred images and expressions of theology – be they models of pastoral agency – shepherd, pastor, priest – metaphors for the ideal Christian life – soldier, servant – or concepts articulating the nature of God – Lord, Father, King – speak to us most powerfully of the implicit values and power-relationships to which the Christian community subscribes. This may not be problematic for those who believe that Christian values are unchanging; but the truth is that they are historically and culturally conditioned, and that the language of the Church's pastoral ministry offers a graphic account of its prevailing models of human nature and destiny, the action of God in the world and the role of the church in the work of salvation.

## The Sexual Politics of Pastoral Care

The use of shepherding imagery to encapsulate the Church's understanding of pastoral leadership and agency is therefore a clear example of metaphors from another age enduring into the modern era. Other aspects of pastoral care through the ages have been recognized as representative of more clearly historically conditioned and culturally specific norms. For most of the Christian era, a primary motif of pastoral care was that of pastoral discipline. The guidance and formation of the individual was seen in terms of demarcating the boundaries of the believing community, which was held to be absolute in its authority, both in dispensing the means of grace and salvation, and defining the terms of their mediation to the faithful. The authority of the ordained clergy stemmed partly from their sociological status as an educated person in the community, and, often, as a representative of an influential and wealthy patron. However, it was also derived from their theological and ecclesiological standing as the representative of God's law on earth through the Church mediated by Word and Sacrament.

Admittedly, Christian pastoral care has also been influenced by the nonconformist impulses of individual conscience, the liberating word of Scripture and the communitarian witness of the New Testament; but the dictates of institutional religion in the name of the claim that there can be 'no salvation outside the Church' have tended to be pre-eminent. This has served to emphasize the collective over the individual in the name of a model of Christian faith, which regards the corporate life of the believing community as paramount. Hence, pastoral discipline places its emphasis on practices which communicate and enforce the standards of the institutional *ecclesia* via practices of confession and absolution, moral examination and strictly administered access to the sacraments. However, this has to be placed in an historical and cultural context which pre-dates modern democratic and egalitarian political ideals, and which places the rights of the individual as subordinate to concepts of the community as ordered according to the tacit authority of tradition and oligarchy.

Judged by the standards of later modernism, which im-

plicitly shapes all our personal and corporate assumptions
and values, this emphasis on pastoral discipline strikes us as
punitive, morally regressive, and autocratic. Modern culture
is founded upon such principles as the universality of
human reason and personal freedom, especially in matters
of religious belief and individual conscience. Thus the
ideals informing notions of human destiny and fulfilment,
and those exercises of pastoral agency deemed necessary to
carry out the will of God do change with time, and the
underlying values informing Christian ministry, in theory
and practice, ought to be subjected to critical scrutiny. Any
pattern of pastoral care, therefore, has to be understood as
a creature of its time and place, reflecting and often enforc-
ing particular cultural norms and values.

## A comparative perspective on culture and history

The implicit values of our time may therefore be more
clearly mapped by bringing them into dialogue with the
taken-for-granted norms of past epochs. The dissonance
and incongruity between past and present sharpens our
attention to the 'horizons' of our own day, as well as
enabling us to identify the temporal continuities.

Such crosscultural comparisons may also be ethnic or
geographical. For example, the pastoral theologies now
emerging from Africa and Asia originate in traditions and
practices established by white Christian missionaries. For
some, this influence represents nothing short of colonization
by Western Christianity, which destroyed indigenous spirit-
ualities and forms of religious expression, and attempted to
impose alien norms and images of Christian vocation and
virtue. Commentators maintain that although some Western
values helped to differentiate the Church from traditional
practices (and in many cases, offering more freedom to
women in terms of greater educational, familial, and economic opportunity), it also prevented the Church from
developing an indigenous theology and spirituality which
would articulate the Gospel in a more culturally appropriate fashion.

Since the early years of the twentieth century, Christian
pastoral care in Britain and North America has been con-

ditioned by the fundamental revolutions in our intellectual and social order, symbolized by the figures of Marx, Darwin, and Freud. Their thinking imbues our attitudes both towards the Christian historical tradition as well as current pastoral practice. If we see the audacity and genius of the earliest Christians in glimpsing and instigating an inclusive and egalitarian human community, it is not simply through the self-evidence of their vision, but also because our sensibilities have been sharpened by the critical perspectives and imperatives of modern socialism, and, more recently, those of feminism and pluralism. Similarly, if nowadays we regard the exemplary pastoral carer as non-judgemental, supportive, and empathetic, that is largely due to the influence of the post-Enlightenment psychologies and psychotherapies which affirm individual autonomy and self-determination as the primary virtues of human fulfilment. Therapeutic models of care in the quest for individual wholeness have replaced what is now seen as a repressive and negative emphasis on sin and conformity to Churchly discipline; furthermore, this is regarded as proof of our generation's moral and theological progress – an idea which is itself a product of the Enlightenment. The extent to which the Christian community should live according to the norms and standards of its time, or adopt countercultural prophetic values, is of course a matter for pastoral and theological debate; but the fact is that pastoral care is neither immune from nor innocent of its social and cultural setting.

## Power and pastoral practice

Pastoral relationships tend therefore to reflect and absorb the prevailing ideals by which norms of human virtue and moral value are judged. Power relations within a wider society – between women and men, black and white, lay and professional – cannot be prevented from invading the sanctuary of the helping relationship. Secular therapies have recognized for some years that the helping relationship can be far from neutral and benign, and that significant scope exists for abuses of power on the part of the counsellor, therapist, or expert. This is true not just in terms of the dynamics of the one-to-one relationship, but to the extent in which both parties are bearers of expectations and prescriptions about what is considered healthy, normal, and good. Pastoral theology needs to be able to reflect critically on the implications of this for Christian pastoral practice.

Norms and ideals inform pastoral strategy by influencing certain choices regarding three main areas of care: questions of agency, priority, and aims and ends. When it comes to examining the norms which inform patterns of who cares for whom and by what means, decisions concerning the needs which merit pastoral attention and judgments on the appropriate virtues to be fostered and wrongs to be righted, it is important to recognize that such choices are not neutral, but have been influenced by already existing value systems.

The changing role of women within the churches highlights the significance of the *sexual* politics of pastoral care. Gender relations are reinforced in and forged by particular models of pastoral ministry. Pastoral care enacts a set of messages about authority and power in the Church, prescriptions for vocation and fulfilment in the Christian life, and understandings of the ways in which knowledge and service of God are attained. All have a critical impact on the treatment of women by the Christian Church: whether the prevailing, however unconscious, objective of pastoral practice is to liberate women, or to restrict them to norms of behaviour and patterns of self-development that serve to maintain male power within the Church.

One of the earliest formative theses of feminist theology illustrates the extent to which the values informing Christian pastoral practice are subject to patriarchal distortion. Valerie (Goldstein) Saiving (1979) argues that the standards of virtue by which the exemplary Christian life was judged ignored women's experiences. To elevate the ideals of service, self-abnegation, and sacrifice may be an appropriate corrective to the patriarchal values of power and domination; but such ideals merely confirm women's subordination and serve to veil the unequal and exploitative nature of gender relations. Anne Borrowdale (1989) has developed this analysis, and illustrated how the Christian vocation to servanthood has become a licence for women's servility and submission.

## Power relations in pastoral agency and pastoral need

The use of images like that of the shepherd to delineate the scope and nature of pastoral care perpetuates models of care which emphasize individualism, professionalism, and directivity. Historically, literature – popular and academic – reflecting on pastoral care has tended to concentrate upon the qualities that characterize the good pastor. Moreover, since its emergence as a specific discipline in the middle of the eighteenth century, pastoral theology has been synonymous with writings on the activity and characteristics of the pastoral agent. For most of Christian history, this also means that pastoral theology so understood implicitly restricts itself to the study of the pastoral agent – traditionally male, ordained, and professionally accredited.

In the process, attention to the needs of the client, or to the dynamics and relationships within the Christian community as a whole, are obscured. Furthermore, the possibilities of other models of pastoral agency – for example pastoral care exercised by lay women – are also occluded, because what is assumed to constitute the normative pattern of Christian pastoral practice reflects the powerful and privileged status of the clergy. The considerable contribution and gifts of women as pastoral agents have been extensively undervalued and unacknowledged. Domestic responsibilities, mothering, and all forms of service have been deemed natural and spontaneous when exercised by women, and therefore regarded as unexceptional models of Christian vocation. There have been many instances of women who have been regarded as harbouring inappropriate, and unfeminine, ambitions by pursuing ministries other than those to the traditional spheres of women's organizations, young people, children and education.

Women are thereby denied autonomy and recognition as pastoral carers; but it is also true that women's pastoral needs are also neglected and misrepresented. Traditionally, pastoral care has been informed by teachings and practices

217

which rest upon the conviction that women's destiny is predetermined by virtue of their supposed connection with natural and maternal qualities. This is understood automatically to preclude them from positions of leadership or autonomous roles in church or society. The destiny and fulfilment of 'good' women rests in the vocation of wife and mother, roles which reflect the 'natural' order ordained by God. Pastoral need is determined in reference to such stereotypes; and pastoral care designed to ensure the inviolability of home and family.

Vital areas of pastoral need for women – questions of abortion, contraception, child care, sexuality, violence and sexual abuse – only began to feature as legitimate pastoral concerns once women achieved greater visibility and entered positions of leadership in the churches. Women's unequal position in society has also gone unchallenged by the churches because pastoral theology has never been sufficiently client-centred to allow such critical perspectives to be articulated.

Thus, both in terms of women's contribution as pastoral carers and in establishing the parameters of pastoral need, pastoral care has served to police and limit the horizons of women, by offering carefully circumscribed role models and visions of selfhood and self-fulfilment. Exclusive concentration on the person and role of the (ordained, male) pastor results in a pastoral theology that neglects the needs of (female) lay people and reflects the value-assumptions of a male hierarchy in ruling on questions of legitimate pastoral need and how to address it; in short, a pastoral theology that is both sexist and clericalist.

## Two models of pastoral theology

The values underpinning pastoral practice therefore embody particular conceptions of pastoral need and pastoral agency. However, they also act as vehicles of pastoral theology as well, in that they serve to articulate notions of the divine through the exercise of care. What the Christian Church considers normative and desirable, and therefore seeks to foster in its life and work – via diverse forms of pastoral practice – is understood as a reflection of the nature of God.

However, such values may actually be rationalizations of ideologies of sexism and clericalism in the name of the divine will. A strategy by which such an implicit theology might be subjected to scrutiny – and restored to a more authentic state – is therefore essential for critical reflection on pastoral practice.

James Griffis (1985) writes about the implicit values which underpin pastoral practice, and argues that there are two distinct and oppositional models available within the Christian tradition. He identifies the tendency within mainstream churches towards what he calls the 'Constantinian' model of care, which embodies principles like control, order and the authority of law. In contrast, he delineates the characteristics of an alternative 'Liberation' model, emphasizing change, *metanoia*, and innovation. Effectively, the choice is between a model of stability and maintenance, against one of liberation and transformation.

The sexist and clericalist model serves in many ways as an example of the Constantinian model: it restricts pastoral agency to male-ordained agents out of an implicit understanding that the grace of God works selectively, through the accredited channels of ordination and privilege. God is regarded as a similarly controlling and authoritative figure; Lord, King and Master of creation, to whom obedience and submission is due. Christian virtue is constituted as conformity to divine authority.

By contrast, a liberative pastoral care takes as its inspiration the prophetic and apocalyptic ministry of Jesus, and a call for conversion rooted in an apprehension of God's transformation of the present via the creative and disturbing activity of the Spirit. Humanity is called into radical obedience to the divine promise for the future, rather than required to preserve the existing order of structure and stasis. Pastoral agency, understood as the prerogative of all God's people, is directed towards the establishment of God's reign of justice and freedom from oppression.

Griffis insists that both models have their virtues: and certainly, the Constantinian model reminds us of the positive aspects of a theology of creation and natural virtue. It also emphasizes the importance of a pastoral ministry that is able to support and sustain those for whom stability and order is a token of the reassuring and consistent love of God at times of acute distress. However, it is also true that to restrict the boundaries of pastoral care to such pacifying and ameliorative functions narrows our ambitions concerning human response to suffering and need, effectively de-politicizing the Gospel and refusing to regard pastoral care as reflecting the challenges of a God who is not only loving but just.

## Feminist theology and pastoral care

Is it possible to see in the paradigm of pastoral practice as Liberation an effective model for the empowerment and pastoral care of women? A commitment to feminist praxis would mean modelling pastoral practice on theological values and insights that promised the empowerment of women and addressed their pastoral needs; but also to see those pastoral relationships as reflections of the divine nature. Christian pastoral practice has the potential to reveal a God who is startlingly present in human encounter. In their relationships and actions of care, Christians believe they can effect some of the creative and redemptive work of God; but that such care will also express something of the divine reality. Thus human pastoral relationships, however expressed, will also be to Christians in some sense a disclosure of God.

The Constantinian model assumes certain avenues for the disclosure and revelation of God, namely the established offices and structures of the Church and officially sanctioned avenues of pastoral practice. The Liberation model, by contrast, understands God to be at work in the faithful action of the poor and outcast in their struggles towards love and justice. A God who inspires such a mission would also inform pastoral practice that engaged in prophecy as well as service: in challenging social structures as well as servicing them; in exercising critical solidarity rather than unquestioning approval. The implications for the pastoral care of women would therefore promote a more proactive ministry, engaging with the structural and political dimensions of women's lives.

Attention to the needs of women in pastoral care alerts us to the reciprocal nature of the pastoral encounter. According to the traditional model, the pastor is the powerful and privileged agent through whom God works, by virtue of their special calling and superior qualities. God is understood to work from a position of strength and power; but this is rather contradicted by liberationist and feminist perspectives, which emphasize the vulnerability of God through the suffering of Christ, and identify the exclusion and pain of the poor and marginalized as experiences through which justice and redemption will be established. The compassion of Christ is thus not a striking of a sympathetic attitude from afar, but literally com-passion, or a suffering solidarity which willingly shares in the limitations of the human condition. Yet the Resurrection is an assurance that the love of God is capable of embracing and transcending finitude and death.

The notion of the suffering God suggests that pastorally God is disclosed as much in the person and situation of the cared for as the carer. What does it mean therefore to talk of a God who is so vulnerable as to be in need of our care, who knows the pain of imperfection and death? It implies a God who enters completely into human affairs, refusing to be abstracted or distanced from the pain of the world. It certainly implies an end to models of care which are based on dualistic relationships of healthy/sick, able expert/powerless client, shepherd/sheep, or ordained/lay; and invites us to consider models of mutuality and incarnate love as paradigmatic to pastoral theology. These are certainly recognizably feminist models, given that movement's promotion of values which emphasizes interconnectedness, mutuality, and relationality.

Finally, such a liberationist model serves to break open our understanding of Christian caring, both in terms of personal agency and the corporate and symbolic nature of pastoral practice. A plurality of models of care are being reappropriated – often deliberately – by women in pastoral situations. Given the social and cultural expectations on women to exercise care – even if, as we have seen, that care goes unrecognized and unrewarded – they come to a closer recognition of the special gifts that caring requires and brings. Here are models and perhaps images that can take their place alongside the established ones of shepherd and pastor to inform Christian caring, and in the process open new avenues and metaphors to apprehend the nature of the divine.

Important developments in deconstruction and literary criticism, as well as critical theory, have informed various perspectives in liberation theology and feminist criticism to suggest that any claim to absolute, final truth involves an occlusion of unvoiced and marginalized perspectives. As we have seen, pastoral care that reflects values of order, authority, and hierarchy functions to bolster the position of the powerful. In the process, it sets limits on our apprehension of God's activity in the world.

By contrast, the Gospel imperative of the bias to the poor involves practising pastoral strategies which empower such silenced groups, and ending those which perpetuate their marginalization. This involves pastoral ministries which not only embody the values of the powerless, but witness to models of truth which refuse the foreclosure of certainty: denying the false divisions and stereotyping (of gender, race, dis/ability, and sexuality) that is born of the 'will to power'. Instead, pastoral values must affirm the mystery and complexity of human nature and the disturbing charism of the Spirit, an ethic of risk and *metanoia*, and thereby temper the more traditional emphases on order, structure, and stability. Thus a feminist pastoral theology necessarily celebrates diversity, heterogeneity, and provisionality, both in terms of human identity and of the possibility of absolute and ultimate truth-claims.

Such an appeal to the provisionality of experience and truth is not to collapse into relativism, or to deny the possibility of truth-claims; but it is to insist that such values can never exist in abstract and are necessarily linked to *praxis*. If pastoral practice is the embodied expression of Christian truth-claims, this means that the Gospel and the Church's mission can never exist independent of the community which enacts and articulates these values. Pastoral care is not therefore the exercise of absolute eternal values, but more the enactment of provisional truth-claims that have to be tested out, in and through Christian practice. As the quotation at the beginning of this chapter testifies, the ultimate benchmark of authentic Christian *kerygma* is the quality of the faith community and discipleship into which the Church calls women and men. Pastoral practice which is directed towards forging authentic and Gospel-related gender relations therefore serves as a crucial instrument of mission available to the Christian community.

This vision of theology is clearly incarnational and sacramental, and this seems consistent with the claims about knowledge, selfhood, and community which feminists have seen fit to make in pursuit of women's emancipation. Tasks associated with the most fundamental, material and embodied human functions form the fabric of the everyday caring roles women have traditionally been required to undertake. As a result, the claims to experience arising from such gendered forms of labour tend to emphasize interrelationality and concretion as the fundamentals of selfhood and community – values often at odds with the dominant Western cultural ethos of autonomous, independent, atomistic individuals. Part of the oppositional project of feminism has therefore been to stand up for notions of the integrated and interrelated nature of human selfhood, which refuse the dualism and individualism of Enlightenment rationality. Similarly, feminist theory refuses the abstractions of empiricism and objectivism, which claim that truth and knowledge are in some way independent of the practices and subjects which generated them.

Such an appeal to the inseparability of knower and known, fact and value, theory and practice, reminds us that all knowledge, including theology, is contextual and situated, unable to abstract and divorce itself from the needs and interests of its generating community. Just as scientists are increasingly regarding scientific knowledge as the product of the social and human practice of doing science, so, too, all theology may be seen as pastoral, originating in the practice of the faith community. Such knowledge originates and returns to 'the present, the particular and the concrete', generated and tested in the crucible of Christian praxis, informed by values and norms themselves already forged as a result of situated and purposeful human pastoral encounters.

The challenge of women to pastoral care does not, therefore, simply require their inclusion in a tradition that remains otherwise unchanged. Instead, it is a programme for reconstituting the nature of pastoral values and the theological understandings which underpin Christian practice. Feminist evocations of difference and diversity eschew models of care which represent control and coercion; but open new avenues of discovering divine truth as provisional and situated. Such values must be grounded in the reality of human community, in order to ensure their integrity and authenticity, and this may be done by rerouting such values back into pastoral practice as the human and embodied enactment of ultimate truth claims. Just as feminist theory challenges the traditional dualisms of theory and practice, body and spirit, emotion and reason, general and specific, truth and contingency, so such a model of theological truth defies the old conventions which claim that principles and eternal truths can be abstracted from the life of the communities which proclaim and enact them. Instead, there is the possibility of a theological sensibility which roots Christian values in the immediacy and concretion of interpersonal encounter, while witnessing to the paradox that at the very heart of such a dynamic of need and response is felt the transcendence which carries us beyond the knowable and certain into the realms of divine disclosure.

REFERENCES

Borrowdale, A. (1989). *A Woman's Work: Changing Christian Attitudes*. London, SPCK.

Crawford, J., and Kinnamon, M., eds (1983). *In God's Image: Reflections on Identity, Human Wholeness and the Authority of Scripture*. Geneva, World Council of Churches.

Griffis, J.E., ed. (1985). 'Theology and Pastoral Care'. In *Anglican Theology and Pastoral Care*. Wilton, CT., Morehouse-Barlow.

Saiving, V. (1979). 'The Human Situation: A Feminine View'. In C.P. Christ and J. Plaskow, eds *Womanspirit Rising: A Feminist Reader in Religion*. New York, Harper & Row.

# Conclusion

Do not cling
Let me be bigger than your
Heart can hold
Rise with me
To a larger vision.

This poem (Lewin, 1990), reflecting on the experience of
women at the Resurrection, speaks of God's larger vision
for humanity. It may find resonance with those who seek a
larger vision of pastoral care, to extend beyond 'women's
concerns' in traditional models, to a fundamental questioning of the core assumptions and values underlying the
process of caring itself.

One principle that has guided the writing and preparation
of this book is that pastoral care is a collective and collaborative exercise; thus the contributions reflect a number of
perspectives, rather than the views of one individual alone.

Concluding comments can do little more than weave
together some of the many themes explored within this
collection, which is also inevitably limited by our own
horizons of race, class, and culture. Yet it is out of this
detailed experience – for individuals and communities –
that it is possible to discover new styles of personal, social,
pastoral, and theological change.

## Pluralism in Women's Lives

One of the fundamental contributions women can make to
theology is to affirm and value diversity and pluralism, both
in terms of process and content. The mixture of stories,
letters, poetry, liturgy and academic discussion in this book
illustrate the diverse ways in which the contributors have
explored new definitions of pastoral care and practice.
Likewise, the diversity within this collection forms part of a

much wider tapestry of women's experience. While all of the contributors understand their situation to be attributable to aspects of their gender, there would be considerable differences in the ways that individuals would analyse and change their situation. Some, for example, would sit more lightly to the label of feminist than others.

All of the contributors locate the starting points of their spiritual journey within the Christian tradition. Although they come from the majority of mainstream Christian denominations in Britain, they reflect a variety of stances, ranging from those who remain active within church structures, to those whose spiritual exploration takes them beyond the institution.

Similarly, the contributors have been affected by the changes in women's self-understanding which have taken place in British culture in the last twenty years. The increasing emphasis on the value of women's autonomy has created an uncomfortable and often painful tension for those within a Christian tradition, which is still essentially patriarchal.

Thus the contributors reflect different positions along a spiritual spectrum, perhaps most sharply illustrated in the conversations between mother and daughter. They explore how a relationship which incorporates both dependence and autonomy can provide a means of developing an authentic spirituality, in which trust and freedom are respected and preserved.

Some contributions explore aspects of racial and cultural pluralism. The letters written by the three single women to each other describe how social attitudes across the cultures make it difficult for women in different geographical and political circumstances to develop a sense of their autonomy – yet they also recognize that single women challenge many social expectations of women's value and worth.

The contributor who describes the problems for women returning to work identifies a clash between the domestic and the public realms. She emphasizes how women returners may find their experience and training subtly discounted by the norms of a predominantly male working environment. This underlines the importance of networks of support, in order to overcome the isolation women experience.

A consideration of potential models of care may often ignore the realities of caring relationships that already exist. The contributor who explores alternative patterns of women's sexuality argues that such hidden traditions illustrate a variety of experiences already present, especially in secular culture, and that a future vision for women is by no means monochrome.

Two consequences of such pluralism are particularly striking. One is that it challenges any attempts to stereotype understandings of what it means to be a woman. Thus the contributors offer a variety of strategies for change, and a range of caring models and resources for doing pastoral theology which may complement each other. The second consequence is one of recognizing both unity and diversity. This entails developing an analysis which both recognizes the complexity inherent in women's differences, yet affirms some common goals in building a vision of the theory and practice of care.

## A Vision of Justice

Celebrating diversity should not be an excuse for lapsing into a comfortable complacency. This book has described some of the most taken-for-granted aspects of caring taking place in undramatic circumstance; yet it has also pointed to areas of considerable stress, both for individuals and groups of women within our society.

Two examples of the personal stress involved are provided by the descriptions of a new mother caring for her child, and the single woman caring for her elderly mother. Both graphically illustrate the personal paradoxes and the many emotional contradictions involved in caring. The new mother argues that mothering gives many women little choice but of self-renunciation, a value also shared with the single woman caring for her elderly mother. Both comment on the ways in which the demands of private caring can create considerable isolation for carers, and both illustrate how voluntary care – all too often women's care – is frequently performed without recognition of the costs involved for those who carry it out.

At the moment, debates about care in the community are part of more extensive changes in the British welfare state; thus there are wider implications for the future of social policy. A detailed exploration of this is not within the scope of this book, nor the expertise of our contributors. But contradictions remain, and may be epitomized by some of the experiences of women working as paid carers within our society. One such contradiction is illustrated by the tension between caring and service which operates when race, class, and gender combine to create multiple disadvantage. Drawing on the experiences of black women working in some sections of the health service, one contributor argues that the care that one section of our society receives may operate at the expense of others who service them.

Pastoral care is thus not an individualized and privatized activity. It takes place within a political context: of debates about the distribution of resources, the aims and goals of caring, the links between different sections of our society, and about the ways that people value one another individually and collectively.

If pastoral care with and for women is to be effective, it needs to take seriously the links between the personal and the political, and to recognize a context of caring beyond the immediate and personal. While respecting women's individuality and uniqueness, it also needs to recognize the underlying social forces which affect their individual well-being and health, and, if neccessary, to challenge and change them.

## Care and Context

Greater awareness of women's experience has implications for our understandings of the way in which care is offered. Throughout this volume, we have implicitly argued that Christian pastoral care extends beyond the boundaries of the Church as an institution, and thus needs to be sensitive to the social context in which it is practised.

The contributor who explores the dilemmas of her role as a social worker describes the tensions she experiences in the goals of caring between care and control. She further argues that there is a conflict between middle-class and working-class values, which are apparent in the assumptions upon which care is organized and offered in the community. Two other articles take up this theme, but in the context of paid ministry on behalf of the Church. They focus on the practice of pastoral care within a culture which does not necessarily accept the authority of the Church. The contributor who explores aspects of working in an industrial culture argues that women working there are often offering unrecognized forms of care, and illustrates how gender stereotyping militates against their appropriate acknowledgement. Likewise, the contributor who writes of her experience as a woman minister in an urban priority area illustrates how churches may represent alien values to those in the community. She argues that some of the qualities of mutuality and relationship enacted within the culture offer Christians new symbols of caring and transcendence.

## A Vision of Wholeness

Several contributors argue that wholeness and redemption are central values for Christians in understanding pastoral theory and practice. However, understandings of these concepts need to extend beyond the personal and individual in order to take seriously the social causes of suffering in specific contexts.

One contributor who explores aspects of women's sexual abuse illustrates how cultural attitudes may perpetuate a climate that blames women for their own suffering. If social assumptions and attitudes about the family perpetuate a climate of abuse, then they need to be rethought. Healing needs to be enacted in changing attitudes which may perpetuate injustice.

A second contributor integrates understandings of artistic creativity, spirituality, and sexuality. She highlights how institutional constraints may distort personal development and discourage an honest exploration of personal identity. In promoting a prescriptive and conformist model of sexuality, churches are in danger of losing the opportunity to learn from the variety of sexual experience, to accept such lifestyles as God-given, and to see them as a legitimate expression of human destiny.

The reality of a distorted world is not only experienced in our attitudes to sexuality, but in the process of nurturing life itself. A third contributor reflects that her experience as a Western mother, for all its contradictions, is brought into sharp relief when recognizing the suffering of mothers and children who are victims of famine in Africa. This is an imperative to repentance and action, in a world that is broken and finite.

These articles resonate with a fourth, linking models of care to understandings of liturgy, language, and symbol. We need to move beyond understandings of pastoral care which rescue the victim to those which offer an understanding of God involved in and standing alongside those who suffer. Those who are the victims of injustice need to rediscover their strength and dignity: individually, politically, and theologically.

## Some Implications for the Churches

If one goal of pastoral care is to recover women's strength and autonomy, it is important to recognize the consequences for the Christian community: in terms of the training it offers for ministry, and the resources it brings to the task from the Christian tradition.

The contributor who explores ministerial training provides evidence that women may develop a confidence problem in preparing for ordination. Gender-related understandings of authority, service and ministry combine with the lack of opportunity in future employment to deskill many women and to empoverish their contribution to the churches. This article resonates with that by the contributor who explores some of the roots of women's insecurity experienced in education. Here, the tensions which women experience, between living for others and the pursuit of academic work, may often result in their underachievement. Yet, paradoxically, if women are to be effective carers they need to be realistic about both their strengths and weaknesses in order to enable others to develop their potential.

Such potential also affects and is affected by the biblical tradition. One dimension of pastoral care encourages

women to tell their story. The contributor who explores the
function of narrative sets contemporary women's stories
against those to be discovered in biblical tradition, to show
how each changes and transforms the other.

Narrative is a potent force for change because it engages
the imagination and thus integrates the intellect and the
emotions in a holistic way. This quality is also true of
liturgy, since it often acts at a precognitive level. The
contributor who explores how worship relates to the experiences of giving birth discusses the ways in which it may
help or hinder women in the process of healing. In order to
be effective for women as an instrument of pastoral care,
she argues that worship needs to incorporate both the
strengths and vulnerabilities of women's experience.

## A Vision of Reciprocity

The contributor who reviews the academic discipline of
pastoral care argues that it is a creature of its time and
place. What happens within any specific pastoral encounter
between givers and receivers of care cannot be isolated
from broader power relationships within society. Feminist
contributions to the discipline recognize that caring is never
value-free, and challenge understandings based on a lack of
mutuality between carer and cared-for. Instead, most of our
contributors emphasize the values of interdependence and
reciprocity, challenging the traditional notion of the invul-
nerability of the carer.

Strategically, and paradoxically, the process of changing
values in pastoral care often involves women articulating
their experience independently of men, in the company of
each other. Just as our contributors would identify themselves differently in relation to feminism, so they would
differ in their attitudes to separatism. It is likely that the
majority would see this as a means rather than an end in
achieving a greater sense of identity and support. Yet
women's insights and attitudes to pastoral care need to be
heard and received by men if our humanity is to be recreated
alongside one another as equals.

Within this volume there will be much that may implicitly
challenge men's experience; but to describe how such atti-

tudes might change would be inappropriate. To do so risks reversing the ways in which sexism has operated for women in prescribing how they ought to behave and respond, and place women in another set of care-taking roles towards men.

Many of those who have contributed to this volume have described the process of caring rather than being cared for. Yet all the contributions recognize those who are receivers of care – be they professionally described as clients, patients, or members of congregations – have as much to teach the experts as any theoretical analyses of their situation.

Although this volume recognizes the value and importance of appropriate professional expertise in the process of caring, several contributors comment that professionalism needs to recognize that a creative use of power restores a sense of dignity and appropriate relationship to those who may be on its receiving end.

## Future Directions

This collection emphasizes that pastoral care is the responsibility of the whole of the Christian community. It can take place in a variety of contexts and in a wide range of styles. It is extremely important that this fact be more fully recognized and supported within the life of the Church. Failure to do so is to devalue the secular vocation of the laity in matters of pastoral care and Christian mission. This has implications for patterns of education and training for Christian ministry, lay and ordained, professional and voluntary.

The recent decision of the Church of England Synod to admit women to the priesthood offers a further opportunity for women to exercise innovative models of pastoral care. However, those traditions which have been admitting women into full, ordained ministry for a generation or more are still uneven in their acknowledgement and support of women in ministry. Despite our reservations about an exclusively clerical paradigm in pastoral ministry, the role of Christian leadership, especially ordained professionals, is crucial if the Church is to begin to shift its presuppositions about the nature of pastoral care.

## Conclusion

Many of our contributors plead for changes in attitudes towards women and pastoral care, for new images to depict the pastoral relationship, and new standards and norms to guide pastoral practice. It is to be hoped that this book will go some way towards exploring some of these alternatives. However, this needs to be accompanied by the provision of resources which make such innovations possible. In particular, we would welcome greater support – in terms of financial resources and strategic planning – for women and men working in difficult and pioneering areas.

Often the greatest challenges to Christian pastoral care arise within communities which are demoralized and isolated as a result of contemporary social policy. Pastoral carers, be they men or women, are subject to considerable pressure in these situations, but require a range of skills and resources – personal and material – for which their training and professional development often leaves them ill-equipped. Thus, the identification of new realms of pastoral need may entail a re-evaluation on the part of the churches of their patterns of preparation and continuing support for ministry.

The underlying premise of this collection has been that the emergence of feminism has generated a new sensitivity to the role of women, and the significance of gender relations in the giving and receiving of pastoral care. Yet this is part of a wider context in which many of the central assumptions of care and welfare in our society are under scrutiny: the nature of professional accountability; the emergence of new forms of acute pastoral need; debates about the funding and organization of service delivery; and the appropriate balance between prevention and cure. As the churches seek to develop new patterns of pastoral care, they will find much to learn from other caring professions and agencies – in health care, community work, social services, and the voluntary sector – who are also seeking to assess and respond to a growing awareness of the dynamics of gender, race, and class upon the provision and delivery of care and welfare services.

In preparing this collection of essays, we are very aware of the support and encouragement that we and all our contributors have received from many un-named friends, members of families, colleagues, and relations. All have encouraged and enabled this initial exploration of women and pastoral care to come to fruition. We hope it stimulates other women involved in giving and receiving care to articulate their experience. For it is when words become flesh that new visions can be created and enacted.

REFERENCE

Lewin, A. (1990). "Easter Morning". In *By The Way*. Winchester, Optimum.

## Further reading

PERSPECTIVES ON WOMEN'S LIVES TODAY

Beechey, V. and Whitelegg, E., eds (1986). *Women in Britain Today*. Milton Keynes, Open University Press.

Llewelyn, S. and Osborne, K. (1990). *Women's Lives*. London, Routledge.

Reid, I. and Strata, E. (1989). *Sex Differences in Britain* (2nd edn). Aldershot, Gower.

Tong, R. (1989). *Feminist Thought: A Comprehensive Introduction*. London, Unwin Hyman.

Clark, D., ed. (1991). *Marriage, Domestic Life and Social Change*. London, Routledge.

Gittins, D. (1992). *The Family in Question: Changing Households and Familiar Ideologies* (2nd edn). London, Macmillan.

Babuscio, J. (1988). *We Speak for Ourselves: the experience of gay men and lesbians* (2nd edn). London, SPCK.

Clark, W., ed. (1987). *Sexuality: A Reader*. London, Virago.

Breen, D. (1989). *Talking with Mothers*. London, Free Association Books.

Rich, A. (1991). *Of Woman Born: Motherhood as Experience and Institution*. (2nd edn). London, Virago.

Arditti, R., Klein, R.D., and Minden, S., eds (1984). *Test-Tube Women: What Future for Motherhood?* London, Pandora Press.

Miles, A. (1991). *Women, Health and Medicine*. Milton Keynes, Open University Press.

Oakley, A. (1985). *The Captured Womb: history of the medical care of pregnant women*. Oxford, Blackwell.

Richardson, D. (1992). *Women, Motherhood and Child-rearing*. London, Macmillan.

Apter, T. (1990). *Altered Lives: Mothers and Daughters During Adolescence*. Brighton, Harvester Wheatsheaf.

Friday, N. (1977). *My Mother, My Self*. New York, Delacorte Press.

Stanworth, M. (1983). *Gender and Schooling* (2nd edn). London, Routledge.

## Further Reading

Weiner, G., ed. (1985). *Just a Bunch of Girls: Feminist Approaches to Schooling*. Milton Keynes, Open University Press.

Coyle, A. and Skinner, J., eds (1988). *Women and Work*. London, Macmillan.

Firth-Cozens, J. and West, M., eds (1990). *Women at Work: Psychological and Organizational Perspectives*. Milton Keynes, Open University Press.

Ford, J. and Sinclair, R. (1988). *Sixty Years On: Women Talk about Old Age*. London, Women's Press.

Lonsdale, S. (1990). *Women and Disability: The Experience of Physical Disability Among Women*. London, Macmillan.

Martin, E. (1989). *The Woman in the Body*. Milton Keynes, Open University Press.

Richardson, D. (1987). *Women and the AIDS Crisis*. London, Pandora.

Brian, B. et al., eds (1985). *The Heart of the Race: Black Women's Lives in Britain*. London, Virago.

Cobham, R. and Collins, M., eds (1986). *Watchers and Seekers: Creative Writing by Black Women*. London, Women's Press.

Phillips, A. (1987). *Divided Loyalties: Dilemmas of Sex and Class*. London, Virago.

Walker, A. (1985). *In Search of our Mother's Gardens: Womanist Prose*. London, Woman's Press.

Dobash, R.E. and R.P. (1992). *Women, Violence and Social Change*. London, Routledge.

Stanko, E. (1985). *Intimate Intrusions: Women's Experience of Male Violence*. London, Routledge.

WOMEN, CARING AND SOCIAL POLICY

Burden, D. and Gottleib, N. (1986). *The Woman Client: Providing Human Services in a Changing World*. London, Routledge.

Dale, J. and Foster, P. (1986). *Feminists and State Welfare*. London, Routledge.

Glendenning, C. and Millar, J., eds (1992). *Women and*

*Poverty in the 1990s.* Brighton, Harvester Wheatsheaf.

Briggs, A. and Oliver, J., eds (1985). *Caring.* London, Routledge.

Lewis, J. and Meredith, B. (1988). *Daughters Who Care.* London, Routledge.

Pitkeathley, J. (1989). *It's My Duty, Isn't It? The Plight of Carers in our Society.* London, Souvenir Press.

Ungerson, C. (1987). *Policy is Personal: Sex, Gender and Informal Care.* London, Routledge.

Chodorow, N. (1978). *The Reproduction of Mothering: Psychoanalysis and the Sociology of Gender.* Berkeley, University of California Press.

Eichenbaum, L. and Orbach, S. (1982). *Outside In, Inside Out: Women's Psychology: A Feminist Psychoanalytic Approach.* Harmondsworth, Penguin.

Ernst, S. and Maguire, M., eds (1987). *Living With the Sphinx: Papers from the Women's Therapy Centre.* London, Women's Press.

Flax, J. (1990). *Thinking Fragments: Psychoanalysis, Feminism and Postmodernism in the Contemporary West.* Berkeley, University of California Press.

Walker, M. (1990). *Women in Therapy and Counselling: Out of the Shadows.* Milton Keynes, Open University Press.

WOMEN AND THE CHURCH

Borrowdale, A. (1989). *A Woman's Work: Changing Christian Attitudes.* London, SPCK.

—— (1991). *Distorted Images: Christian Attitudes to Women, Men and Sex.* London, SPCK.

Carr, A. and Fiorenza, E.S., eds (1991). *The Special Nature of Women?: Concilium 1991/6.* London, SCM Press.

Edwards, R.B. (1989). *The Case for Women's Ministry.* London, SPCK.

Franklin, M.A. and Jones, R.S. (1987). *Opening the Cage: Stories of Church and Gender.* Sydney, Allen and Unwin.

Furlong, M. (1991). *A Dangerous Delight: Women and Power in the Church.* London, SPCK.

McEwan, D., ed. (1991). *Women Experiencing Church: A*

## Further Reading

*documentation of alienation.* Leominster, Gracewing.

Miles, M. (1988). *The Image and Practice of Holiness: A Critique of the Classic Manuals of Devotion.* London, SCM Press.

FEMINIST THEOLOGY AND SPIRITUALITY

Hampson, D. (1990). *Theology and Feminism.* Oxford, Blackwell.

Loades, A., ed. (1991). *Feminist Theology: A Reader.* London, SPCK.

King, U. (1990). *Women and Spirituality: Voices of Protest and Promise.* London, Macmillan.

Ruether, R.R. (1992). *Sexism and God-Talk.* (2nd edn). London, SCM Press.

Thistlethwaite, S. (1990). *Sex, Race and God: Christian Feminism in Black and White.* London, Geoffrey Chapman.

Byrne, L., ed. (1991). *The Hidden Tradition: Women's Spiritual Writings Re-discovered.* London, SPCK.

Gray, E.D., ed. (1988). *Sacred Dimensions of Women's Experience.* Wellesley, MA., Roundtable Press.

Plaskow, J. and Christ, C.P., eds (1989). *Weaving the Visions: New Patterns in Feminist Spirituality.* San Francisco, Harper & Row.

Quaker Women's Group, (1986). *Bringing the Invisible into the Light.* London, QHS.

Fiorenza, E.S. (1984). *Bread not Stone: the Challenge of Feminist Biblical Interpretation.* Boston, Beacon Press.

Russell, L.M., ed. (1985). *Feminist Biblical Interpretation.* Oxford, Blackwell.

Morley, J. (1992). *All Desires Known* (2nd edn). London, SPCK.

St Hilda Community, (1991). *Women Included.* London, SPCK.

Sears, M. (1989). *Life Cycle Celebrations for Women.* Mystic, CT, Twenty-Third Publications.

Stuart, E. (1992). *Daring to Speak Love's Name: A Gay and Lesbian Prayer Book.* London, Hamish Hamilton.

Walker, B.G. (1990). *Women's Rituals: A Sourcebook.* San Francisco, HarperCollins.

## Further Reading

NEW PATTERNS OF PASTORAL CARE

Fischer, K. (1989). *Woman at the Well: Feminist Perspectives on Spiritual Direction*. SPCK.

Glaz, M. and Moessner, J.S., eds (1991). *Women in Travail and Transition*. Minneapolis, Fortress.

Milhaven, A.L., ed. (1991). *Sermons Seldom Heard: Women Proclaim Their Lives*. New York, Crossroad.

The Mudflower Collective, eds (1985). *God's Fierce Whimsy: Christian Feminism and Theological Education*. New York, Pilgrim Press.

Cooey, P.M., Eakin, W.R., and McDaniel, J.B., eds (1990). *After Patriarchy: Feminist Transformations of the World Religions*. New York, Orbis.

Fabella, V. and Oduyoye, M.A. (1988). *With Passion and Compassion: Third World Women Doing Theology*. New York, Orbis.

Halkes, C.M. (1991). *New Creation: Christian Feminism and the Renewal of the Earth*. London, SPCK.

Kanyoro, M.R.A. and Robbins, W.S., eds (1992). *The Power We Celebrate: Women's Stories of Faith and Power*. Geneva, World Council of Churches.

O'Neill, M. (1990). *Women Speaking, Women Listening*. New York, Orbis.